Can't We All Just Get Along?
Resolving Baseball's Civil War

Dean Wilson

YorkshirePublishing
www.yorkshirepublishing.com
Write Now

Can't We All Just Get Along?
Copyright © 2019 by *Dean Wilson.*

ISBN: 978-1-949231-92-2 (Paperback)
ISBN: 978-1-949231-93-9 (Hardbound)

Yorkshire Publishing
4613 E. 91st St.
Tulsa, Oklahoma 74137
www.YorkshirePublishing.com
918.394.2665

Dedication

To my wife, Sara:
For your constant, unwavering and unconditional love and support in all that I do, even when it requires you to sacrifice yourself in the process. It's an absolute joy to share life with you.

Mom:
For never, ever missing a single detail, no matter how small, and for always sacrificing yourself for those around you, especially your family. You are the most selfless person I know.

Dad:
For being there for every up and down, every step of the way, and always pushing me to stray from my comfort zone to try new things. You're my hero and main droog for life!

Aunt Motherre:
You and Mom-Mom always used to tell me to, "kick ass!" So, here goes nothing! Thanks for being my second home.

To family, friends, teammates, players and coaches:
Thanks to some for encouraging, some for doubting, but thanks to all for your unique impact on my ongoing journey, no matter how small or large. Barrington to Brookdale to Tulsa, I hope to make all of you proud with every endeavor.

Contents

Introduction

B aseball is a game rooted in tradition. From the religious observing and enforcement of the unwritten rules to the pre-game national anthem and everything in between, baseball holds its traditions extremely close and values respect and recognition of those who came before in the utmost esteem. With that being said, baseball is also a game in the midst of a revolution the likes of which would make King George III assume the fetal position. The war cry of, "Make baseball fun again," echoes through clubhouses and stadium concourses alike (for what it's worth, I've always thought baseball was fun), and stats like wOBA, wRC+ and WAR have become to forward-thinking front office executives what Batting Average, Slugging Percentage and RBI are in the minds of baseball traditionalists. While you may be asking, "Isn't change a good thing? Wouldn't finding new ways to see the game be beneficial?" The answer to that question is yes.

And no.

Baseball is a game with so many variables and moving parts present in every single pitch, that of course constantly refining and tightening up the lens through which we view the game is a great thing. However, the (allegedly) antiquated line of thinking did the job for over 100 years, and is now being slowly pushed out by the new regime, citing that it is becoming obsolete. Regardless of side, progressive or traditional, both lines of thinking have a movement behind it as ravenous as the other, hell-bent on proving the other wrong, emerging victorious and standing alone at the top of the mountain, intellectually superior. As much as all people in baseball rely on each other in order to have success, this type of conflict caught me off guard and has always struck me as atypical for baseball people.

Understand, I recognize that human nature is such that tribal instincts exist in even the smallest fibers of our DNA, and the need to join the crowd and fight the opposing powers, regardless of how small the battle will exist in the psyche of man for generations to come. However, it has been my experience that any success in baseball is a collaborative effort. During my time in baseball as a player or coach, I've never witnessed someone climb the ladder completely on their own. I've never seen someone achieve and reach the pinnacle of their profession, baseball or otherwise, solely on their ideas, their practice routines, their theories and their execution. The merit of the individual in question may be there, and they may be the one who shoulders the vast majority of the load when it comes to their success, but reaching a certain level of success in any area of baseball is generally achieved through a blending of theories. Hear a lot of ideas from a lot of different people, keep what makes sense, ditch what doesn't and voilà, there is your outlook on the game. So, for the last several years, to sit back and watch grown men, and highly respected baseball people, essentially engage in the old schoolyard:

"I'm right."

"No, I'm right!"

"No, I'm right and you're stupid," makes me cringe. This is a kid's game, yes, but that's no excuse to be stubborn and stomp your feet like one. There's a place in this game for everyone and every theory, given that it's able to be proven in some way to be legitimate. The traditional approach to the game has it merits, and the progressive approach has its place. Both have benefits, both have flaws and both have their place in this game. Regardless of what you subscribe to as of your opening of this book, it is my hope to prove to the masses that Batting Average doesn't suck, bunting is okay, wOBA isn't a new brass instrument and Range Factor is just how many plays you make per nine innings. Nothing is anything by which to be intimidated or to be looked down upon. I've always found that being open to all possibilities is the best way to learn, there's always someone out there smarter than you. On the off chance that there isn't, a new perspective can still be a game-changer in terms of your ability to be effective at what you do. I have found this to be true over the course of my life in the game, and that is, in part, why I find myself so drawn to baseball.

If I may get personal for just a moment, I'd like to talk about why I came to love baseball in the first place. Baseball, in my humble opinion, is the greatest sport and one of the greatest developers of character that humankind has to offer. It's such a different game than nearly all of the other sports in the world, especially the main American sports. Most other sports are your standard two-goals-at-each-end-whoever-scores-the-most-by-the-time-the-clock-hits-0:00-wins style format. Some are just on grass, some are on ice, some are on hardwood, and the size and shape of the object being used to score differ, but the object and play of the game overall remains the same.

Baseball is different. There is no clock. You can't take a knee or dribble it out and milk the clock. You have to get in there and get the other guy out 27 times. If you can't do that, you don't win. Legendary manager Earl Weaver once said, "In baseball, you can't kill the clock. You've got to give the other man his chance. That's why this is the greatest game," and that has always resonated with me. No checking the clock, no stalling, just you and the guy standing across from you. No way out but to engage in the battle. I love that. Put up or shut up, if you can't finish the job yourself, the job doesn't get done and I think it's the purest form of competition.

Baseball is different. There is no "team," per se. There are nine guys in the lineup every night (10 in the American League, thanks DH!), but one of my favorite parts of baseball is that there's only ever one man representing the whole team at any given moment. One pitcher with the ball. One hitter with the bat in his hands. One defender to field the ground ball and one teammate to catch the throw. There are no route trees or pick and rolls. In fact, the closest thing baseball has to organized team maneuvers is the hit and run, and if one of the guys doesn't do their job, the play is kaput. I love that there's only ever one player that's on the biggest stage, representing the entire roster. No higher high, and no lower low, and it's an opportunity unique to baseball.

Baseball is different. It's a game rooted in failure. If a quarterback in football completes 30% of his passes, he'll be holding a clipboard by next week. If a basketball player shoots 30% from the field, guess who's not getting the ball at the buzzer? If a goalie saves 30% of shots on goal, they'll heckle him asking why he has those big fluffy gloves if he doesn't use them. In baseball, if a player gets a hit 30% of the time, he's a Hall of Famer. Is that a direct testament to the fact that baseball is harder than other sports? Not necessarily. However, it is a testament to the toughness and mental fortitude necessary to be a successful baseball player or successfully maintain your sanity while being a fan of the game in general.

Baseball is a beautiful game. It's a kid's game that, at the highest level, is played by adults. It's the kind of game that builds men, but allows them to continue being children simultaneously. It creates a dichotomy between the harshness of adulthood and innocence of children, all while fastballs are whizzing by your head at 96mph. Poetry. Baseball is such a tremendous game because it's so difficult. Difficult to play, difficult to understand.

Which is why it drives me absolutely insane that everyone so desperately wants the world to know that they have all the answers!

How arrogant is it to believe that your way of looking at the game is even the right way, let alone the only way? The advances in kinesiology, motion capture technology, mathematics and algorithm development, etc. allows us to, almost on a yearly basis, see the game in a whole new light. So, how can anyone think they know *anything*, let alone *everything*? It baffles me. You know nothing. And guess what? Neither do I, let's talk about it! That in itself is the beauty of the whole thing.

In no way do I promise this book to be a manual by which people should develop their theories on baseball. Nor do I assert myself as a foremost authority on anything. What I do hope, though, is that I can use my experiences through my years playing and coaching the game to shed some light on some of the things we baseball people quibble about on a daily basis. I'm looking to introduce a unique perspective of the way baseball is viewed, analyzed and discussed. I find myself to be one of the few people who aren't wholly a traditionalist or wholly a sabermetric progressive. I'm not sure if it's the ego of man that allows them to, in their own mind, never be wrong or to avoid changing their mind like it's the plague, or if perhaps there are really 10 to 15 baseball savants on every sports network who truly know all there is and I'm just a simpleton, wandering through life, blissfully ignorant and hopelessly stupid. I think the jury may still be out on that one.

There are far too many theories, too many ideas and too many brilliant baseball people working on them for us to simply brush any of them off and declare them unfit for our consideration. There is an obligation of all committed baseball people to accept all the information out there about the game, at the very least, until one has decided that it bears no use to them. Simply shutting any way of thinking out is shortsighted, firstly, but also disrespectful to the game. To assume that one's way of seeing the game is the end all be all of views and one's mind is objectively the most beautiful of all baseball minds is asinine. Baseball is hard enough as it is. It's hard to play, hard to manage and hard to nail down and quantify, so the divisiveness of today's game is only broadening the gap.

Baseball people need to come together and see the benefits and drawbacks to all ideas, theories, strategies, analytics, etc. if we ever want to get the most out of the game. There is a civil war raging, and all that ever does is push people further apart. The best hitters in the game only get a hit 30% of the time, so if not everyone agrees with your idea, you're not alone in obscurity. But that's not an excuse to shun a whole faction of the game, behind the scenes of which thousands of incredibly brilliant minds are working to look at the game more effectively.

In this book, I will attempt to both prove and disprove aspects of the traditional line of thinking as well as the new-age mindset. I will draw parallels between popular measures of talent and production that wouldn't even make eye contact if they saw each other in the street. In other words, it is my aim to unite the people through coming to an agreement that all types of stats, approaches and theories have their place, to end all the constant argument and debate that exists in our game today. Above all else, it's my aim to ask one question of the many brilliant and capable minds who share this beautiful, sweet science we call baseball:

Can't we all just get along?

PART 1
Benefits Of Traditional Thought

O ld habits die hard, but that doesn't mean we should keep trying to kill them. As mentioned before, baseball is a game that highly values tradition. Some of the people who hold such traditions dearly are very protective of these traditions and, like an alpha wolf keeping an eye on the maturing males of the pack, are very wary of newcomers to the block.

To others, a lot of times it's more like the old man down the street yelling, "Get off my lawn!" But I digress,...

The game of baseball is incredibly reliant on statistics to tell the story of players' on-field production. For over a century, basic percentage statistics ruled and were the standards by which a player was measured. In recent years, the quality and reliability of these have been called into question. A large portion of this argument is based on the fact that these statistics don't give a broad enough look or offer enough insight on what the player is truly producing on the field. However, I would argue that that is not necessarily their aim. Baseball is a very complex game that can, at times, be broken down into very simple terms (see *Bull Durham*'s famous quip: "You catch the ball, you throw the ball, and you hit the ball!"). It is my belief that these stats don't aim to give an all-encompassing look into the inner-workings of park effects or era-based metrics. Batting Average just wants to tell you what percentage of at-bats end in a hit and RBI just want to tell you how many runs scored as a result of Johnny Smith hitting the baseball.

Pulitzer Prize nominated writer David Foster Wallace once said, "Clichés earned their status as clichés because they are so obviously true." In that vein, the same goes for the traditional statistics that have become staples of player analysis and development. These measures have lasted for so long because they, for the most part, do a good job of explaining what they are designed to explain.

Baseball analysts have been attempting to create and introduce new statistics since the game's inception. Some of them stick and some of them don't pan out, much like the many players that have played on the game's largest stage. Everyone is trying to find newer and better ways to look at the game, but newer and better are not always necessarily the same thing. Traditional outlooks on the game have lasted so long because teams and players have derived value from them in some form or another.

With that being said, not all of the traditional angles at which the game is viewed are as beneficial as others, and some of them have remained a part of the game much to the chagrin of modern analysts, but such is the case with anything. There is good, there is bad, and they are not mutually exclusive. We as baseball people must weed through all the information to truly find what works and what doesn't, not simply discredit something because we don't like it on the surface. Old stats have their benefits just as much as any new ones.

Granted, to say that these stats are enough to provide the finest details in a world where players' pre-game bowel movements may be quantified into a weighted metric would be silly. However, if examined properly and with the correct context, I've found that traditional statistics often tell a similar story to the new-aged ones, albeit in a different, potentially less detailed way. However, the key is to understand that's not why they exist. Let's spend a little time digging into these "antiques" and try to extract some value, even given the landscape of the modern game.

Chapter 1
Baseball's Old Faithful:
The Benefits of Batting Average

I don't think there is a statistic that drives loyal sabermetricians crazy quite like Batting Average. It's the simplest measure of baseball performance, yet it is slandered as heavily as any other attempt to quantify a player's contributions. The main assertion against Batting Average is that it is too simple, it doesn't dig deep enough or tell the whole story behind a player's ability, either current or projected. While this may be true, it's also not the point. As previously stated, it's simply a percentage of AB (at-bats) that end in a hit. Too simple? Possibly, especially in today's "closer look" baseball culture. But, unreliable? Not necessarily.

The main assertion of the new regime, as evidenced by its mention in the film *Moneyball*, that detailed General Manager Billy Beane's analytic approach to building his Oakland Athletics team for the 2002 season, is that On-base Percentage (OBP) is king. Then, why is Batting Average not an important statistic? The primary means by which a player reaches base is via hit, thus making Batting Average the majority of any player's OBP. For those that don't know, OBP is just the percentage of Plate Appearances (not just at-bats, as is the case with Batting Average, so OBP takes into account at-bats as well as trips to the plate that end in BB, HBP, and sacrifices) that result in the player safely reaching base, with the exception of intentional walks (IBB). They're essentially the same statistic, one (OBP) just measures more than the other. Batting Average is simply hits divided by AB and On-base Percentage is Batting Average, just with the addition of BB, HBP and sacrifices to both sides of the equation. They're so similar, yet one has been crowned king, while the other has found its head placed securely in the guillotine. OBP measures more overall, yes, but that doesn't change the fact that Batting Average is the primary factor in OBP.

If you look at the numbers, hits are a lion's share of plate appearances that end in a player reaching base safely, even for the players with the keenest mastery of the strike zone.

Of the players with top 50 BB (base on balls or "walk") totals in Major League Baseball in 2017 (the last completed season as of this writing), none of their walk totals exceeded their hit totals. Joey Votto of the Cincinnati Reds, who is widely known as one of the best in the game at drawing walks, walked 134 times in 707 plate appearances in 2017, which was the highest total in Major League Baseball. His OBP was .454, also tops in the game. However, he also tallied 179 hits in 559 at-bats, producing a Batting Average of .320. Clearly, his Batting Average accounts for a greater portion of his OBP than anything else. In an effort to quantify Batting Average's impact on OBP, we will separate the components of OBP and tally them separately.

OBP consists of hits, BB and HBP (hit by pitch). You take that total, then divide the number by the total number of PA, or Plate Appearances (at-bats + BB + HBP + sacrifice fly). The sacrifice fly is important because a sac fly will actually lower a player's OBP. So the end formula is:

$$OBP = \frac{H + BB + HBP}{AB + BB + HBP + SF}$$ [1]

SF is sacrifice fly. So, for these examples, we've separated hit total from BB/HBP and divided them by both AB and PA individually. Dividing by AB will produce a Batting Average equivalent and dividing by PA will provide an OBP equivalent. Essentially what we're looking to do is to see what would happen if a player's hit total and BB and HBP total, respectively, were to stand alone and be the number by which both Batting Average and OBP were calculated. The difference between the two totals should give us an indication of how significant

---

[1] Formula via FanGraphs

the hit total, i.e. Batting Average is in a player's overall production. Expect "adjusted" Batting Averages and OBPs of hit totals to be much higher than that of the BB/HBP total. This will demonstrate the impact that Batting Average has in comprising OBP.

JOEY VOTTO - 2017				
BB/HBP	*At-bats*	*Batting Avg.*	*PA*	*OBP*
142	559	**.254**	707	**.201**
Hits	*At-bats*	*Batting Avg.*	*PA*	*OBP*
179	559	**.320**	707	**.253**
Difference		**+.066**		**+.052**

As you can see, even if you take all the outcomes other than hits that can positively affect OBP (walk, hit by pitch), the best OBP in the league is still most heavily influenced by hit total. In other words, Batting Average plays. Taking a player's hit total and calculating Batting Average and OBP (As if hits were the total number of PA's in which the batter reached safely), and doing the same with BB/HBP, the hit total's BA and OBP were 66 and 52 points higher, respectively. For some reference, 66 points of Batting Average is the difference between Albert Pujols (.303, 100.2 career WAR[2]) and Aurelio Rodriguez (.237, 15.2 career WAR) and 52 points of OBP is the difference between Tony Gwynn (.388, 69.2 career WAR) and Dante Bichette (.336, 5.7 career WAR). To clarify, WAR stands for "Wins Above Replacement" and is the crown jewel of the analytics movement. It accounts offense, defense, base running, park effects, era weights, etc. to provide a number that demonstrates how many more (or less) wins a player produces for his team than the league average player.

I know I used WAR in the traditional section of the book, which may cause some baby boomers to close the book immediately, but stay with me; it's simply a means of further illustrating the parity between my examples. We'll get into WAR later.

---

[2] WAR data via Baseball Reference

Knowing how frequently a player gets hits tells a large portion of the story in regard to how often they reach base safely, which is the name of the game in addition to, obviously, scoring runs (but you can't score if you record an out every PA). Let's compare Votto's numbers to the 50th highest walk total in 2017, and someone who more profoundly demonstrates the impact of Batting Average of On-base Percentage, the Colorado Rockies' Charlie Blackmon.

CHARLIE BLACKMON - 2017				
BB/HBP	*At-bats*	*Batting Avg.*	*PA*	*OBP*
75	644	**.117**	725	**.104**
Hits	*At-bats*	*Batting Avg.*	*PA*	*OBP*
213	644	**.331**	725	.294
Difference		**+.214**		**+.190**

Charlie Blackmon led the league in hits (213) and Batting Average (.331) in 2017. In addition, his OBP of .399 was still good enough for 12th in all of Major League Baseball, despite walking only 65 times, which was, again, 50th in the league. His hit total by itself would have been good for a .331 BA and .294 OBP, while his BB/HBP total would have had a BA of .117 and OBP of .104 if left to stand alone as the full total of times Blackmon reached base safely. The difference in OBP would be equivalent to that between the career marks of Ted Williams (.482, 123.1 career WAR) and Dal Maxvill (.292, 7.7 career WAR). The difference in Batting Average would be comparable to the distance between Ty Cobb (.366, 151.1 career WAR) and an offensively pedestrian pitcher (.152 Batting Average). Keep in mind, Williams and Cobb are the all-time leaders in MLB history in OBP and BA, respectively. So the fact that Charlie Blackmon's hit totals account for such a larger percentage of his reaching base should show the value that hits, and in turn Batting Average, have in terms of distinguishing how much a player is getting done. If you get hits and don't walk, you're still generally going to have a decent On-base Percentage.

I've shown a high-hit and high-walk player (Votto) as well as a high-hit and low-walk player (Blackmon). For my last example, I will use Odubel Herrera of the Philadelphia Phillies, who is not a bad hitter, but not getting hits at the pace of Blackmon or Votto, and who walks notoriously seldom.

ODUBEL HERRERA - 2017				
BB/HBP	*At-bats*	*Batting Avg.*	*PA*	*OBP*
35	526	.067	563	.062
Hits	*At-bats*	*Batting Avg.*	*PA*	*OBP*
148	526	.281	563	.263
Difference		+.214		+.201

As we can see by looking at Odubel Herrera's breakdown, his hit total also makes up an enormous piece of his overall OBP. His OBP for the 2017 season was .325. With percentage points excluded, we see that his hit total makes up approximately 80.6% of his On-base Percentage. The same can be said for Charlie Blackmon, with his hit total accounting for 73.7% of his total OBP. Joey Votto, being the BB-drawing virtuoso that he is, still saw over 55% of his OBP comprised of only hits.

These numbers also stay fairly consistent as a career rate. 76.7% of the plate appearances in which Herrera reaches safely come via hit, with Blackmon's career number being very similar, at 76.9%. These numbers do not stray far from their output in 2017. Joey Votto, as if it's any surprise, has stayed consistent as well, with a career total of 60% of his OBP being due to hits. The numbers show definitively that getting hits has far more to do with OBP than anything else. And if that is the case, with OBP being as large an indicator of value as it has come to be, then it stands to reason that a high Batting Average should play a pivotal part in determining a player's value. For many players, $^3/_4$ of the PA in which they reach base safely end with a base hit, and for the elite BB earners, like Joey Votto, that number ends up being closer to the $^3/_5 - ^2/_3$ range. Joey Votto has led the league in BB in six of his 12 full Major League season, and has led the league in OBP seven times.

However, if he were just a slightly less successful hitter, it would be a different story.

If Joey Votto had as many hits as BB/HBP in 2017 (142), which is 37 less hits than he actually tallied (179), and which ends up being around 1.5 less hits per week for a whole season, the numbers dramatically change. His Batting Average would obviously drop, from .320 to .254. His OBP, which is tops in the league by 10 points over OBP leaderboard mainstay Mike Trout, and 51 points higher than number 10, Freddie Freeman of the Atlanta Braves, would drop below both of them. If Joey Votto had 142 hits, his OBP would drop to .402, one point *below* Freeman, causing him to fall out of the top 10 altogether. Losing one and a half hits per week can take a league leader and make him a sub-top 10 finisher. The value of hits on OBP is significant, and due to that, Batting Average and its impact on OBP should be recognized and valued.

I'm not entirely sure the day in which we as a collective baseball community decided that we were no longer worried about players getting hits and the frequency with which they were able to do so. And don't say, "We don't think that, Batting Average is just outdated!" If Batting Average is outdated, so is getting hits at a high clip being instrumental in determining the ultimate value of a player. You have to get hits to win games. Only twice in the history of baseball has a team been no-hit and won the game, once in 1964 and once in 1967. Obviously, a team could never win if a perfect game is thrown against them, because no batters reach base. In addition, no one has ever seen a player hitting .330 and said, "That guy sucks."

What I'm trying to say is that a team needs to hit to win, and therefore getting hits is important. By that logic, if getting hits is important, and getting them frequently enough to push across runs is important, then Batting Average should matter, shouldn't it? It's the only statistic that measures solely the frequency with which players get hits.

I'm not mad at people saying the guy with the highest Batting Average shouldn't necessarily be given the title "Batting Champion," because I understand that there is more that goes into batting than simply getting hits. However, I've never heard anyone call a player who gets a lot of hits a bad hitter. Is Batting Average as involved as some of the newer metrics that we'll unpack in the rest of this book? No. But that's no reason to cast shade on a timeless classic.

At the end of the day, getting hits is the name of the game. The game revolves around hits. You won't score runs if you don't get hits, and you don't win games if you don't score runs. If that is the case, and OBP is an industry staple, wouldn't the primary contributor to a player's OBP be a stat worth noting? Batting Average is not archaic, it's classic. A throwback that measures one of game's most common and simultaneously most sought after commodities, hits. Even if you're an analytically-inclined person, all hits are weighted heavier than BB and HBP in the wOBA formula (we'll get to that later, as well). All that says is that hits are what it's all about. Batting Average may not differentiate between different types of hits, but one needs to get hits before worrying about what kind of hits they're getting. Batting Average provides the answer. When looking at a player, we see: A) Guys who have a high Batting Average get a lot of hits relative to their at-bats. B) Guys who have high Batting Averages typically have a high OBP. C) Guys who have a high OBP are extremely valuable. Therefore, logically, Batting Average is extremely valuable.

If a=b and b=c, then a=c. Numbers don't lie (looking at you, data analysts), and neither does the Transitive Property of Equality. It *is* math, and we like math! Right?

Chapter 2
The Big Payoff of Small Ball

E very high school coach's favorite play is also the bane of every devoted analytician's existence, but you know it as the bunt. More specifically, the sacrifice bunt. Giving up an out to advance a runner in an effort to place them in a more favorable position to score. The numbers indicate that generally, bunting decreases overall run expectancy. However, those who have to sit in the dugout and answer for wins and losses can tell you that *expected* runs are significantly less important than *actual* runs, because expected runs don't go on the scoreboard. The following visual was taken from FanGraphs about RE24 or "Run Expectancy based on 24 base-out states," [pause to breathe] which indicates the expected runs for an inning based on every possible base occupancy combination:

Runners	0 outs	1 out	2 outs
Empty	.461	.243	.095
1 - -	.831	.489	.214
- 2 -	1.068	.644	.305
- - 3	1.426	.865	.413
1 2 -	1.373	.908	.343
- 2 3	1.920	1.352	.570
1 - 3	1.798	1.140	.471
1 2 3	2.282	1.520	.736

Order is 1st base (left) 2nd base (center) 3rd base (right) 1= 1B, 2= 2B, 3= 3B, "-" means
no runner occupying that base

To read this chart, an example would be that, "1 - -, 0 out" is runner on first only, with 0 outs. That situation in any given inning can be expected to yield .831 runs. "- 2 3, 1 out" is runners on second and third with one out. A team in that situation could expect to come away with 1.352 runs in that inning. So, now that we are equipped to understand what we're looking at, let's take a look at the situations.

From a strictly expected run standpoint, sacrificing an out for base position is never an improvement. However, as I stated previously, in the bottom of the ninth when your team is in the midst of a tie game or losing by one run, you're not trying to score as many runs as possible for that inning, you're trying to score one run. And in the case of scoring only one run, waiting for the percentages to even out in your particular instance is often futile. He who hesitates…

In my playing and coaching experience, I have found that at lower levels, bunting is definitely over-used. However, I've found that at the higher levels, bunting may be *under*-utilized. I understand that the game is such that we generally wait around for a three-run homer to provide our scoring, but there are times which call for a small-ball play in an effort to simply push one run across with the game on the line.

According to Jeremy Frank, founder of www.ngbaseball.com, the three most common final scores in Major League Baseball history (totals as of this writing) are as follows:

1.) **4-3** (11,976 occurrences, 5.7% of all games)
2.) **3-2** (11,560 occurrences, 5.5% of all games)
3.) **2-1** (9,771 occurrences, 4.7% of all games)

That's a total of just under 16% of all games, or just under $\frac{1}{6}$ of every game ever played in the history of Major League Baseball has ended with a final score of 4-3, 3-2 or 2-1. The difference one run makes in a baseball game is significant. In fact, an extremely large portion of all MLB games have ended in a one-run victory. Over the course of MLB's history, there have been approximately 210,000 games played. Of those, 63,548 of them have been one-run games. That's approximately 30.3% of *all* games in the history of Major League Baseball, which dates back to the 1800s. Nearly one-third of all games are decided by one run. With that knowledge, wouldn't bunting in that situation be wise in an effort to avoid the same fate that befell 63,548 losing teams before them?

Well, if you're so smart, why don't you tell us how an extra base can help score that extra run?

With pleasure! Generally, I'm not a fan of bunting from first base to second base. As evidenced by the chart provided earlier, we know that a runner on first with 0 outs holds an expected run value of .831 runs, while a runner on second with one out holds an expected run value of .644 runs. Obviously, that is a smaller number, so not the best play. However, the main reason I'm not a huge fan of it is that with a man on first or second, you still generally need to rely on a hit to score the runner. I'm of the opinion that in order to sacrifice an out, one needs to be put in a position where they have many different opportunities to score than they had prior. To me, bunting is extremely valuable in late-game situations when moving a runner from second base to third base.

One of the main reasons I'm a proponent of the second base to third base bunt is that there are many more ways to score from third with less than two outs than from second, barring some sort of freak occurrence. To name a few:

-   Balk
-   Wild Pitch
-   Passed Ball
-   Infielder error
-   Sacrifice fly
-   Suicide or Safety Squeeze
-   Steal of home

In addition to those, there are often times when a hard-hit single that lands in front of an outfielder is too well-hit to score a runner from second, but would score the runner from third. Also, if the infield is playing back (which in a high-leverage situation, they probably would not), a routine ground ball out will also score the runner from third.

The potential benefits to bunting don't end with creating different ways to score. There are also somewhat intangible benefits to bunting effectively. One of these effects is putting pressure on the defense.

But, how does plopping a ball 30mph, 30 feet away from home plate put pressure on the defense?

Because anybody can watch a home run sail over their heads, but not everyone can field a bunt.

How many times have you seen a third baseman charge a ground ball, throw on the run and sail one into the third row behind first base? How many times have you seen a catcher come out from behind the plate, spin and throw off-balance and the ball ends up rolling into the right field corner? How many times have you seen a pitcher try to lob the ball all of 15 feet to the first baseman and airmail it so badly that the launch angle would make Red Sox slugger, J.D. Martinez blush? A bunch of times, to all three. Now let me ask you this: How many times have you seen an outfielder rob a home run that lands 10 rows up in the left field seats? Never. Not to say bunting is more valuable than home runs, because I would never say that as I don't agree with it. I will say, however, that in a pinch, a bunt is a far higher percentage play and a better way to create some chaos. Take, for instance, a couple teams that won the World Series while relying heavily on the sacrifice bunt to jump-start their offense.

In 2006, the Cardinals were managed by legendary manager Tony LaRussa, who is notorious for his propensity for playing "small-ball." His 2006 World Series champion team was no exception. In Major League Baseball that season, they ranked 12th in HR (184), 15th in Slugging Percentage, or SLG (.431) and 14th in runs per game (4.85). They also had a 4.54 team ERA, which was 16th overall in the MLB rankings to go along with the 10th highest Fielding Percentage in the league (.984). The one category that they were top-10 in was [drumroll please] sacrifice bunts, in which they ranked ninth (71).

Now, am I saying they won their division and ultimately the World Series solely by bunting? No. But I am saying that they weren't good enough on the mound to rely on pitching alone, they didn't hit enough to wait around for three-run home runs, so they had to score somehow, and it would appear, based on Tony LaRussa's M.O. throughout his career, that was to bunt and put pressure on the defense.

Another good example is the 2010 World Champion San Francisco Giants. This was the first championship in a three-in-five-years run that had some fans crying dynasty. However, they didn't swing the bats like some of "Murderers' Row" Yankees teams which were surrounded by the same talks of dynasty. Granted, maybe those Yankees teams were a bit more star-studded with Babe Ruth and Lou Gehrig on the same field, but three titles in five years is still tough to dispute.

In 2010, the Giants ranked 10th in MLB in HR (162), 13th in SLG (.408) and 17th in runs per game (4.3). Unlike the '06 Cardinals, however, they were elite on the defensive side of the ball. The Giants' pitching staff boasted a league-best 3.36 team ERA and a .988 team Fielding Percentage, which was fourth in Major League baseball. In addition, guess what other statistic they were top-five in? That's right, sacrifice bunts, in which they ranked third with 76 [3].

This was a team that, again, couldn't adopt the Earl Weaver model to winning baseball games ("Pitching, defense and the three-run home run,"). However, they came close with the pitching, defense and sac bunts edition. They threw strikes, made plays and put pressure on the defense because they weren't going to make it rain long balls all season. So, if anyone says that you have to hit home runs to win baseball games, tell them that's not true, and tell them I sent you.

I think the reason that this model plays out so frequently in favor of the small ball teams in the postseason is that it's so hard to hit home runs consistently when you face teams that have elite pitching staffs. It's harder to sit back and wait for three-run home runs when 1) You can't hit that many home runs due to great pitching, and 2) There's not that many runners on base due to great pitching. When that is the case, it's very difficult for teams who rely on the home run to score runs

[3] Baseball Reference

consistently. Waiting for a great pitching staff to have four off nights out of seven is often an exercise in futility. Bunting allows a unique way to put pressure on the defense, speed the game up and force a team to take part in making plays that, by October, haven't been thought much about in the seven months since Spring Training.

Again, if you take averages and expected run values, bunting is not an option. But if you have a situation where you need a hit to score a runner with no outs, or can score nearly 10 additional ways with one out, expected runs go out the window. Either you *do* score, or you *don't* score. They won't ask what the run expectancy was in the post-game presser. Bunting is not the savior of baseball and the solution to a team's run-scoring problem. However, there is a definite place for the bunt in baseball and completely abandoning it is a mistake. Walk-off homers are great TV, but managers and players don't get bonus checks for high Nielsen ratings.

Chapter 3
Stolen Bases Slide, Safely, Under the Radar

A nother lost art in the modern game is the stolen base. Many forward thinkers would point to the graphic used in the bunting section as proof that stolen bases are simply not worth the risk. A man on first with no outs tries to steal. If he's safe, the increase in odds that his team scores a run is actually sometimes less than the decrease in odds if he's thrown out. In other words, the general consensus from the modern baseball minds is that the reward of being safe is not generally worth the risk of being out. However, I would disagree. In a game when 30% success is the gold standard, one would think taking 70+% odds to increase run scoring potential would be a no-brainer. Granted, not being smart about stealing bases is essentially giving away bases – and outs – but if done efficiently and with consistency, the overall production of a player can be shown to be increased markedly. As an example, let's use some of the game's most prolific base stealers.

Everyone knows Rickey Henderson was a masterful base stealer; his 1,406 career stolen bases are 468 more than his closest competitor and, with the significant dip in stolen base attempts since the "go-go" days of the 1980s, his is a mark that may stand for a long time, if not forever. He stole 100 bases in a single season three times, with his single-season record 130 bags coming in 1982. In other words, it is safe to say Rickey knew what he was doing on the base paths.

Yes, he's the all-time leader in SB, but he also is the all-time leader in caught stealing!

Dean Wilson

He sure is! Just like Nolan Ryan is the all-time leader in strikeouts *and* walks… yet he still boasts a greater than 2:1 strikeout to walk ratio. Rickey Henderson has been accused of being a *volume base stealer*, one that simply runs all the time with no regard for consistency or running his team out of innings and this is simply not the case. Rickey Henderson has a career SB% (stolen bases divided by total stolen base attempts) of 80.8%, which is actually 47th all time. I know 47th may not sound like a lot, but the list only requires 80 career SB attempts, and Henderson has nearly 600 more stolen bases than the next closest career total in the top 50 all-time (Tim Raines, 808 SB, and his 84.7% is 12th all-time). The point being, he was only thrown out so much because he ran so much. The averages would indicate that despite all the caught stealing (CS), he was still an extremely effective base stealer before you even factor in the freakish amount of bases he actually stole successfully. In an effort to quantify the value of stealing a base despite the possibility of being thrown out, I'm going to try something a little different.

What I'm going to do is account for the number of times Henderson turned a single into a double (stealing second base) or turned a double into a triple (stole third base). He actually even turned a triple into a home run four times by stealing home, but none of that really matters until I explain *why* it matters. I will assess these extra bases on Henderson's batting statistics, as well as assess his CS as if they were batted outs to see if the risk is really worth the reward. I will be using both traditional and analytical measures to present the data, so bear with me!

Rickey Henderson had a career Slugging Percentage (Slugging Percentage is total bases, so 1B=1, 2B=2, 3B=3 and HR=4, divided by at-bats and is used to measure a player's power production. So higher the SLG, more power the player hit with) of .419. 4,588 total bases in 10,961 career AB. Let's take a look at how that number changes when assessing the benefit of SB and the detriment caused by CS.

Total Bases:	SB	New Total Bases	New SLG	Difference
4,588	1,406	5,994	.547	+128
Total Bases:	**CS**	**New Total Bases**	**New SLG**	**Difference**
4,588	335	4,253	.388	-31

Clearly, the value Henderson added by stealing bases vastly outweighs the harm he caused by being thrown out 335 times, even though it is more than any other player has been thrown out in history. His stolen bases added 128 points on his Slugging Percentage in that he added 1,406 extra bases to his offensive game simply by stealing them instead of hitting for them. A .547 career slugging percentage is just 3 points shy of Alex Rodriguez's career total, for reference. If you count only the negative effect from his caught stealing, his SLG would drop only 31 points, to .388. That SLG would be comparable to that of Davey Lopes, no stranger to the stolen base himself (557 career SB), current coach and a 16-year MLB veteran with over 1,600 career hits.

At the end of the day, stealing or hitting, bases are bases and scoring position is scoring position, regardless of how one gets there. It reminds me of a seemingly unrelated story my dad told me when I was younger that made me fall in love with infield defense, but the more I think about it, the more it directly applies to the point I'm making:

Hall of Famer Ozzie Smith is an all-time Cardinal great and the greatest defensive SS to ever walk the earth, which is the one thing I will not debate in this book. Despite that, he was never regarded as a huge offensive threat, although he did become a good hitter later in his career.

In 1985, he signed a lucrative (for that era, nobody was getting $300-million deals in the '80s), multi-year contract which included an eventual base salary of over $2 million for the 1988 and 1989 seasons. For reference, the two comparable contracts to that point in time were those of Mike Schmidt and George Foster, who both also reportedly received annual salaries of approximately $2 million.

Foster was a pivotal piece of the Cincinnati Reds' "Big Red Machine," which won two World Series Championships and averaged over 95 wins per season for the entirety of the 1970s, and is widely regarded as one of the best teams in the game's history. Foster was a member of all of those teams except the 1970 edition, and he made his presence felt. He was named National League MVP in 1977 when he hit 52 HR and tallied 149 RBI. He finished his career with 348 HR.

Schmidt was one of the most feared sluggers of his time, and widely regarded as one of the best all-around third basemen ever. He was inducted into the National Baseball Hall of Fame in 1995. He finished his career with 548 HR, hitting 35 or more in 11 different seasons, winning three National League MVP awards while appearing in 12 All-Star Games in his career. So, the kind of players that were receiving $2 million salaries at that time were some of the most feared sluggers of their day, and Ozzie Smith got paid like them.

All despite being only a .238 career hitter to that point in his career.

When the concerns about the high value of the contract, despite Smith's light offensive production, were brought up to then-manager Whitey Herzog, he justified the signing by saying, "I don't care if he doesn't drive in 100 runs a year, he saves more than 100 runs a year with his glove." On another occasion, he said, "If he saved two runs a game on defense, which he did many a night, it seemed to me that was just as valuable to the team as a player who drove in two runs a game on offense."

The reason I bring that up is because, in Herzog's opinion, runs saved equals runs produced. Whether they're kept off the board or added on, they affect the bottom line the exact same way.

When thinking about Henderson's contributions of extra bases due to his tremendous base-stealing prowess, I thought of those quotes by Herzog and it reminded me that just as is the case with runs prevented vs. runs produced, bases hit for and bases stolen both put the team the same 90 feet closer to scoring a run. It doesn't matter if he drives the ball in the gap for a double, or if he walks and steals second. No matter how it happens, Rickey's standing on second base, and if you get caught napping, he'll probably be on third before the inning is over. Henderson exemplifies that concept as well as anyone. Still not satisfied? Let's venture into the new world and see how this same principle affects Henderson's wOBA (weighted on-base average.)

wOBA is a linear-weights metric used to determine a player's overall offensive contribution. It works by attributing an expected run-based weight to each potential outcome. The formula is:

[4]

$$wOBA = \frac{.69 \times uBB + .72 \times HBP + .89 \times 1B + 1.27 \times 2B + 1.62 \times 3B + 2.10 \times HR}{AB + BB - IBB + SF + HBP}$$

Some editions of wOBA also add a weight to reaching on an error. Essentially, the formula values a BB at .69 runs, a HBP at .72, a single at .89, etc. Henderson's career wOBA is .372, which is very good. However, it is lower than his overall value due to the fact that with the bat in his hands, he hit mostly singles (2,182 singles out of 3,055 total career hits). However, once on first, he was very rarely held to just one base. What I've done is added the times he's stolen second base, third base and home to his doubles, triples and home runs and, in a separate experiment, subtracted his CS at each from those same hits. After this, we can examine just how much value his base thievery produced.

	1B	2B	3B	HR
Total # of hits	2,182	510	66	297
SB	0	1,080	322	4
Equivalent # of hits	1,102	1,590	388	301
New wOBA: .438		*Difference*: +66		

Henderson was 1,080-for-1,338 stealing second base, 322-for-391 stealing third base and 4-for-12 stealing home.[5] As you can see, the value of the extra bases he created by stealing (turning singles into doubles, doubles into triples, etc.) increased his wOBA by 66 points. Taking him from already well above average .372 to an exorbitant .438. You'll also notice that somehow his singles total dropped, that's not because he was

---

[4] FanGraphs
[5] Jeremy Frank, www.ngbaseball.com, Twitter: @MLBRandomStats

thrown out trying to steal first base. I added his 1,080 steals of second base to his doubles total, but also subtracted them from his singles total. I did this because he was giving up his position at first to attempt to obtain better position at second base. Had I left his singles total at 2,182, his wOBA would have increased all the way to an other-worldly .511, 139 points above his true career total, and one point higher than Babe Ruth's career mark, which happens to be the best of all-time. For the sake of the argument, we'll leave his assessed singles total at 1,102. Let's take a look at how his historically-high caught stealing numbers detract from his overall production using the same formula:

	1B	2B	3B	HR
Total # of hits	2,182	510	66	297
CS	0	258	69	8
Fewer times on base	258	69	8	0
Equivalent # of hits	1,924	441	56	297
New wOBA: .342		Difference: -30		

So you don't have to do math based on his aforementioned splits, Henderson was caught stealing second base 258 times, third base 69 times and home eight times. If you'll notice, there is an extra row in this chart, allow me to explain. The "fewer times on base" row calculates how many hits are being subtracted from each type of hit. I got this number by finding out how many times Henderson was thrown out attempting to steal the next base. For example, if Henderson was thrown out attempting to steal second, even if he hit a single, it's like he never hit that single because he gave up his position at first by unsuccessfully attempting to steal second. I did the same for stealing third and home. He gave up doubles getting thrown out at third, and gave up triples in an effort to steal home. There's no way to give up home runs, the next step after home plate is sitting down in the dugout, so home runs remained consistent with his career total.

In order to quantify his added value using both risk and reward, you can simply subtract the points lost for being thrown out from the points gained from stealing successfully, and adding the difference on to his true career total. For SLG, His adjusted career slugging would be .516 (128 points added minus 31 points lost = 97 added points. .419 + .097 = .516), which would place him around 65th all-time (he's currently 664th) and ahead of sluggers such as Harmon Killebrew, Jose Canseco and Rafael Palmeiro. In terms of wOBA, his adjusted number would be .408, which is 36 points higher than his true career mark (66 points worth of value, 30 points worth of harm = 36 points total value).

I don't think these calculations are outlandish or farfetched as a means of assessing value of stolen bases. As I mentioned before, bases are bases regardless of how you get there. Scoring position is scoring position, whether a guy hits a double or steals second. No one has ever felt bad and asked to be out when a guy makes an error or an umpire blows a call, and that's because getting on base and advancing bases matter. If a guy can do that effectively, it's clear there is added value in being able to consistently advance the extra base.

So, when it comes down to it, the risk is definitely worth the reward for Rickey Henderson. The value that was derived from his stolen bases, based on wOBA (if you're into that), took him from "Rickey" to somewhere between Barry Bonds (career .439 wOBA) and Babe Ruth (career .510). The detriment due to his being caught stealing drops him to .347, only 28 points lower than his career mark and would still be, according to FanGraphs, considered "above average." His adjusted wOBA was .408, which is two points shy of Giancarlo Stanton's wOBA in 2017 (he hit 59 HR and won National League MVP honors). Stealing bases allowed him to add value similar to that of a feared power-hitter having a career year, despite the fact that Henderson averaged only 46 extra-base hits per 162-game season (27 2B, 3 3B, 16 HR).

If you don't like the Rickey Henderson example, let's try a more human base stealer. Well, not necessarily human in terms of quantity of stolen bases, but rather in success rate. Enter: 18th all-time career base stealer, Juan Pierre.

Pierre stole 614 bases in his 14-year Major League Baseball career, which, as we said, ranks 18th all-time. Despite stealing 792 *fewer* bases than Rickey Henderson, he was only caught stealing 128 fewer times, leaving his career stolen base percentage (SB%) at 75.2 for his career. Pierre had notoriously little power at the plate, hitting only 18 career home runs in over 8,000 plate appearances. As his low HR total would indicate, his career power numbers are far inferior to those of Henderson, as he finished his career with a .361 SLG and a .315 wOBA. Let's take a deeper look and see how much value stealing bases has on a player like Pierre, who consistently had slightly less success stealing bases.

[6]

Total Bases:	SB	New Total Bases	New SLG	Difference
2,714	614	3,328	.442	+81
Total Bases:	CS	New Total Bases	New SLG	Difference
2,714	207	2,507	.333	-28

[7]

	1B	2B	3B	HR
Total # of hits	1,850	255	98	18
SB	0	478	133	3
Equivalent # of hits	1,372	773	231	21
Equivalent # of hits	1,924	441	56	297
New wOBA: .358		Difference: +43		

	1B	2B	3B	HR
Total # of hits	1,850	255	98	181
CS	0	186	15	2
Fewer times on base	186	15	2	0
Equivalent # of hits	1,664	240	96	18
New wOBA: .287		Difference: -28		

His adjusted SLG ended up being .414 (81 points added minus 28 points lost = 53, .361 + .053 = .414). From a wOBA perspective, he increased his wOBA by 43 points by stealing successfully and cost himself 28 points by being thrown out. Adjusting his actual career total

---

[6] Baseball Reference
[7] FanGraphs

based on this would leave his total adjusted wOBA at .330 (43 points added – 28 points lost = 15, .315 + .015 = .330). While it seems he did help his own case by stealing bases successfully, his added value was very little compared to that of Rickey Henderson, proving that stealing bases is only as effective as your efficiency in doing so.

Rickey Henderson stole successfully over 80% of the time, which took his potential value to Bonds-ian altitude, at minimum. Juan Pierre, at 75%, saw his SLG improve, moving him into the low 700s in terms of all-time SLG rank, and while his adjusted wOBA is still classified by FanGraphs as between "Average" and "Above Average," it is still a staggering 78 points below Henderson's adjusted average. Keep in mind, the difference between their actual wOBAs, as would be listed online, is only 57 points. That means that their stolen base success (or lack thereof) actually broadened the gap of production value between them. This could be attributed to either Henderson's being more efficient or Pierre's being less efficient, or both. Efficiency is key!

In addition, you may have noticed that the amount of CS for Juan Pierre added up to be 203, not 207, as indicated in his SLG chart. Baseball Reference indicates that his total career CS is 207, but the total amounts he was caught attempting to steal each base comes out to 203. This is most likely due to pickoffs and other potential instances where he was retired on the base paths that technically go in the book as a caught stealing, but obviously were not an instance of him being thrown out attempting to steal any specific base. Whether the number is 203, 207 or 335, efficiency in stealing bases is pivotal in optimizing the usefulness of actually attempting the feat.

In Tom Tango's *The Book*, it states that, based on the win value of stolen bases, a player needs to be at least 71% successful on stolen base attempts to yield a positive value. Based on our findings here, I would say there is still some value to be had from stealing bases at a 70% clip, but going much lower than that would cause the value to be so miniscule that I wouldn't consider it worthwhile either.

Juan Pierre is 186th all-time in career SB%, at 75.153. So, while he wasn't necessarily an elite base stealer in terms of efficiency, the amount of bases he stole successfully while maintaining a 75% success rate is still impressive. Many players on that list have less than 100 career SB, only running on pitchers with notoriously slow times to the plate and situations where they could exploit a blatant hole in the defense, much like running on a pitcher like Noah Syndergaard in today's game (Syndergaard consistently takes 1.8 seconds to get the ball into the catcher's mitt. For reference, coaches generally encourage pitchers to stay at or below 1.3 seconds). If they were to attempt 821 SB as Pierre had, it is likely that their career success rate would be significantly lower. In terms of overall value, Juan Pierre was an effective base stealer, and stealing bases is an effective and undervalued way to contribute to your team's ability to win games, assuming you're efficient.

Of course, I'm not a fan of blindly stealing bases, as was more prevalent in the 1980s. As backed by Tom Tango's evaluation and the numbers that we ran here, efficiency is key. Somewhere around a 70% success rate is the cutoff point at which a base stealer either contributes or costs his team. With every coach having a stopwatch on pitchers and catchers, knowing runners' straight steal times and modern motion capture technology to catch small tells a pitcher may have as to whether he's picking off or delivering a pitch, teams should have a good idea of the moments in which a successful stolen base attempt is likely. In those situations, teams should put the runner in motion and see how many additional opportunities to score are created.

PART 2
Drawbacks Of Traditional Thought

W hile I don't consider myself anti-analytics, I do consider myself generally pro-traditional when it comes to baseball and its
many traditions. I'd say overall I'm pro-aspects of both and anti-aspects
of both, hence the writing of this book.

Blasphemy!
I hate you!
You can't have your cake and eat it too!

To heckler number two: I'm disappointed, but not surprised. To
heckler number three: watch me. While I do think there is value to
be had and practices that are under-utilized in the modern game, I do
understand that some of the measures by which we rate and evaluate
players are outdated and have glaring flaws.

For the progressively-minded fan or professional, many traditional statistics provide insight, but often times lack context. They do
a good job in their own space, but sometimes are unable to provide a
full in-depth look at player performance. Traditional statistics, while
able to stand alone, often only tackle one specific faction of the offensive, defensive or pitching game at a time. In a world where we need
to know everything a player can do from spin rate to launch angle to
the macronutrients present in the post-game spread, we typically pre-
fer more of a one-stop shop type of statistic. Due to that, a lot of old-
school statistics give a limited look at a player's true performance,

or even totally misrepresent the value that player is truly adding to his team.

So as to prove my neutrality (maybe indifference when it comes to all the in-fighting), I'll outline some of the old-school statistics and practices that should rightfully be moved on from (Hang tight, Moneyballers, you'll get your turn). There are a number of them, but I will try to keep it to only a few.

Chapter 4
Pitcher Wins Take the "L"

P itcher wins, while a staple of pitchers' stat lines and always one of the first three points anyone makes when pleading a pitcher's case for the Cy Young Award, is generally an unreliable measure of a pitcher's effectiveness. It speaks to the ownership and ultimate effect a pitcher has on a game, as he is the one with the ball in his hand, who dictates the pace of the game and who is generally to blame if a team loses. However, it's not a good measure of how well a pitcher is performing in a given season.

I'd like to do an exercise with you. I'm going to show you two stat lines and awards from the 2010 season, and then two W/L records. I'd like you to, using logic, pair those stat lines with the records:

ERA (rank)	FIP (rank)	IP (rank)	K (rank)	WHIP (rank)
2.27 (1)	3.04 (9)	249.2 (2)	232 (2)	1.06 (5)
4.19 (65)	4.25 (70)	176.1 (T-58)	146 (T-48)	1.25 (39)

One of these stat lines has a record of 13-12, the other has a record of 18-8. There is also one Cy Young Award and one All-Star Game appearance between the two of them. Take a minute and think…

Okay time's up. Did your final product look something like this?

Record	ERA	FIP	IP	K	WHIP	Cy?	ASG?
18-8	2.27	3.04	249.2	232	1.06	Yes	Yes
13-12	4.19	4.25	176.1	146	1.25	NOPE	No

Thank you for playing our game, you win nothing! You actually likely proved my point for me, unless you recognized the trap. This is not the way it actually happened. The true lines worked out like this:

Pitcher	*Record*	*ERA*	*FIP*	*IP*	*K*	*WHIP*	*Cy?*	*ASG?*
Hernandez	13-12	2.27	3.04	249.2	232	1.06	Yes	No
Hughes	18-8	4.19	4.25	176.1	146	1.25	No	Yes

That's right, Felix Hernandez was top five in essentially every pitching category, yet still had a record of 13-12. Phil Hughes cracked the top 50 twice in those same statistical categories, yet went 18-8 and was an All-Star, while Felix was not. Granted, Felix won the Cy Young, which was a huge step forward in voters not getting caught up in some of the superficial aspects of post-season award voting (for example: I believe the MVP can play for a bad team; value is value, just because your team stinks doesn't mean you didn't keep them from potentially losing 115 instead of 105), but the fact remains that pitcher wins have much less to do with the actual performance of the pitcher than the performance of the team on days when the pitcher starts.

Of course, there is something to be said for a pitcher's team winning games on the days they start, and I understand that. However, sometimes pitchers simply play for bad teams with anemic offenses, lackluster defenses, poor bullpens or even worse yet, all three, and simply will not get enough help over the course of the season to win a lot of games, regardless of how well they pitch.

In 2010, Felix Hernandez had an ERA (earned run average) of 2.27, meaning he gave up 2.27 runs per nine innings pitched. Phil Hughes had an ERA of 4.19. Basically, if both pitchers threw a complete game every start, opponents of Felix's Seattle Mariners would average about two runs per game in his starts, and Hughes' Yankees' opponents would average right around four. The difference is, in 2010 the Mariners averaged 3.17 runs per game offensively and the Yankees averaged 5.30 runs per game. In other words, Phil Hughes got an average of 2.13 extra runs of support every time he pitched, which certainly would account for the fact the he had 5 more wins and 4 fewer losses than "King Felix." If their records were for a division race, Hughes would be 4.5 games ahead of Hernandez, even though he didn't pitch better in any statistical category *other* than wins. Let's take a closer look into exactly how much Hernandez suffered due to his sub-par team:

The 2010 Seattle Mariners went 61-101, good for last place in the American League West division. The 2010 Yankees went 95-67 in the always-strong American League East and ended up advancing to the American League Championship Series. Despite Hernandez's spectacular season, the Mariners went 17-17 in games he started, while the Yankees went 21-10 in Hughes' starts, despite him giving up nearly two runs more per nine innings pitched than Hernandez. Are we beginning to see how wins are misleading? If you're not convinced, let's try this:

In 2010, Felix Hernandez made 34 starts. Of those 34 starts, 30 of them were what would be considered a "quality start." A quality start is a start in which a pitcher pitches six or more innings, and allows three or fewer earned runs. Of those 30 quality starts, the Mariners lost 13 of them, for a record of 17-13 in his quality starts, with his personal record being 13-8 in those same starts. If you recall, the team's overall record in Hernandez's 34 starts was 17-17, so all four of his non-quality starts resulted in a loss for the Mariners. Long story short, if Hernandez didn't turn in a quality start, the Mariners lost. Even if he did have a quality start, they still lost just less than half the time, 42% of the time to be exact. Hernandez threw 229$^{2/3}$ innings with a 1.57 ERA in his 30 quality starts. He posted 20 IP and a 10.35 ERA in his four non-quality starts.

HERNANDEZ	*Starts*	*IP*	*ERA*	*Team W/L*	*Team Win%*	*Pitcher W/L*
Quality Start	30	229.2	1.57	17-13	.567	13-8
Non-Quality Start	4	20	10.35	0-4	.000	0-4
TOTAL	34	249.2	2.27	17-17	.500	13-12

Hughes on the other hand, fared much better due to the benefit of a quality team. Hughes made 29 starts in 2010, and 15 of them were quality starts. In those quality starts, he pitched $98^{2/3}$ innings with a 2.46 ERA, which is very good, but still a whole run worse than our friend Felix Hernandez, who lived life at .500 all season. In Hughes' 15 quality starts, the Yankees went 13-2, and Hughes went 12-2. In Hughes' non-quality starts, Hughes went $75^{2/3}$ IP with a 6.54 ERA, yet the Yankees still managed a .500 record, going 8-8 while Hughes was 6-6 in those starts. Keep in mind Felix had a higher ERA in his non-quality starts, but he only made four of them. Hughes had a 6.54 ERA over the course of 14 starts, nearly half of his total starts for the season.

HUGHES	Starts	IP	ERA	Team W/L	Team Win%	Pitcher W/L	Pitcher W%
Quality Start	15	98.2	2.46	13-2	.867	12-2	.857
Non-Quality	14	75.2	6.54	8-8	.500	6-6	.500
TOTAL	34	174.1	4.19	21-10	.677	18-8	.692

For more reference, if Hughes played on Hernandez's Mariners, it is possible his record would have been around 10-16. There were eight starts in which Hughes allowed four or more earned runs and the Yankees still won. Keep in mind, the Mariners scored just a hair over three runs per game in 2010. So four runs from the opponent would win the game. That's eight definite games that would have been lost, dropping his record from 18-8 to 10-16, and the teams' record in his starts from 21-10 to 13-18. Now, let's see how Hernandez would have benefitted from having a great team behind him like the 2010 American League runner-up New York Yankees.

Hernandez made nine starts in which he allowed less than five earned runs and still was the losing pitcher. If he had the 5.3 runs per game of support like Hughes had, less than 5 runs allowed would have been enough to win the game. If that were the case, all nine of those starts would have likely resulted in a win for the team and a win on the record of "King Felix." If he had nine additional wins and nine fewer losses, based on his actual record of 13-12, his record would likely have been somewhere around 22-3. His team's record of 17-17 in his starts would have improved to at least 26-8, and all would have been right with the world and I may not have had such a strong case against pitcher's W/L record being thin through the middle.

Hernandez clearly pitched much better over a larger part of the season than Hughes, yet he came away having less to show for it in terms of wins because the rest of his team was unable to produce runs or hold leads once he left the game. Wins aren't a good means by which to measure a pitcher's production, because it relies so heavily on everyone else doing their job. Generally, such is life with baseball, but when dependent statistics begin to affect the way awards and accolades (and contract bonuses) are doled out, something needs to be said.

Speaking of awards, wait, there's more! We haven't even talked about the All-Star Game yet!

If you'll go back to the original charts I displayed, you'll see that despite winning the Cy Young, Hernandez wasn't an all-star and, despite having worse numbers, Hughes was. How could this be? You don't think – *NO* – it couldn't be, did wins play a factor? It would appear that they did.

At the all-star break in 2010, Felix Hernandez had a 2.88 ERA to go along with $137^2/_3$ IP, 7.7 hits/9 IP, 2.8 BB/9 and 8.6 K/9. Phil Hughes had a 3.65 ERA, 101 IP, 8.0 H/9, 2.6 BB/9 and 8.1 K/9. Hernandez had a better H/9, K/9 and only 0.2 more BB/9 in just over 36 more IP. It would have taken Hughes six additional starts given his 6.18 IP/start rate during that season to make up the 36 IP difference, and it is possible his "per 9 IP" rates could have changed in those six starts. To lay it out in a more aesthetically pleasing way:

Player	ERA	IP	H/9	BB/9	K/9
Hernandez	2.88	137.2	7.7	2.8	8.6
Hughes	3.65	101	8.0	2.6	8.1

Even with these numbers as they are, Hughes was an all-star and Hernandez was left off the roster. This is most likely due to the fact that, at the all-star break, Hughes was 11-2 and Hernandez was 7-5. There are really no other factors that aren't either the same or that

Hernandez wasn't better than Hughes. Not to say Hughes had a bad year, or was undeserving of an all-star nod that year. I'm simply saying that if Hughes was an all-star, then so was Hernandez.

To offer another look at how win-loss record can skew the way we look at a pitcher's performance, let's take a look at what has taken place so far in the 2018 season.

As of the writing of this book, the 2018 regular season is not yet completed. However, there is a pitcher's record anomaly taking place in the way of New York Mets' Jacob deGrom. deGrom is currently 8-8 in 26 starts. He also has the league's best ERA at 1.71 as well as 214 strikeouts in 174.0 IP, 2.07 FIP (we'll talk about FIP later) and a 0.971 WHIP (walks + hits per innings pitched). Granted, he is in all National League Cy Young conversations, but it goes to show that a pitcher can pitch as well as a guy can and still have a poor record.

To compare, there is another pitcher in the Big Apple with the opposite issue. He hasn't pitched poorly by any means, but he hasn't pitched as well as deGrom, yet the quality of his team has allowed him to lead the league in wins with 17 to this point in the season. He is the Yankees' Luis Severino. Let's compare the season statistics between deGrom and Severino:

Pitcher	Starts	Record	ERA	FIP	IP	WHIP	ERA+	BB/9	K/9
deGrom	26	8-8	1.71	2.07	174.0	0.971	216	2.1	11.1
Severino	27	17-6	3.27	3.10	165.0	1.139	134	2.2	10.3
+/-			-1.56	-1.03	+9	-0.168	+82	-0.1	+0.8

deGrom's Mets are 58-72, and average 4.16 runs per game, but only score 3.4 runs per game in games that deGrom starts. Severino's Yankees are 83-47 and average 5.2 runs per game and actually score more in Severino's starts, averaging 5.6 runs per game with him on the mound.

To do a similar comparison of the one we did with Felix Hernandez and Phil Hughes, Severino has surrendered four or more earned runs in a start six times. If he had the 3.4 runs/game support that deGrom has, he would not have won those games, and his record likely would have fallen to 11-12. The Yankees average 5.6 runs in Severino's starts. If deGrom got that much run support, knowing that he has given up more than five earned runs *zero* times this season, would he be undefeated? Would he have only won his decisions, going 16-0? At the very least, his record would be far superior to his current 8-8 and likely in line with or better than Severino's 17-6.

Again, not to discredit Severino, he's having a very good year and this is not to take anything away from his accomplishments during the 2018 season thus far. I'm simply attempting to illustrate how a pitcher's record can be misleading. Severino has pitched well, but deGrom has objectively pitched better, yet has a much worse record.

At best, pitching wins/losses is a good measure to determine that a pitcher is leading the charge for a good team, or is toiling away on a poor team, or somewhere in between. What a pitcher's record is not is a way to glean any kind of understanding as to how well they are producing. There are plenty of pitching statistics that are able to quantify a pitcher's contributions, but I think it's important to understand that a pitcher's wins and losses are rarely totally his own to claim or suffer from. With the exception of a pitcher throwing a complete game shutout *and* hitting a home run, a pitcher relies on the other eight players, plus his bullpen to win a game, thus making pitching wins more an indication of how a pitcher's team does during their starts than how the pitcher is doing themselves.

Chapter 5
Putting the "OPS" in "OOPS"

O PS (On base plus Slugging) is a statistic that has made its way into the mainstream in recent seasons. It has been included in TV broadcasts where the standard "Batting Average, Home Runs and RBI" totals had once resided. However, it has found its way into the traditional section of this book because it combines two traditional statistics: On-base Percentage and Slugging Percentage.

If OPS seems simple, that's because it is. To calculate OPS, you simply follow the instructions laid out by the title of the statistic itself: add OBP and SLG. The result is OPS, what some consider a good way to determine both the hitter's ability to get on base and to hit for power.

Those are two very important parts of baseball. So then why, Dean, is this in the drawbacks section of the book?

Well, because simpler isn't *always* better and, mathematically speaking, inaccurate is *never* better, and OPS is both. Allow me to explain.

First off, can someone *please* explain to me what exactly OPS measures? I know it combines On-base Percentage and Slugging Percentage, but those are separate stats, so simply presenting the sum of those two as its own statistic doesn't make a whole lot of sense. Does it measure power production? Does it measure ability to get on base? Realistically, it measures both separately, but not cohesively. OPS doesn't combine OBP and SLG in any explicable or mathematically sound way. It simply takes two existing statistics and stacks them on top of each other and passes itself off as some sort of all-encompassing statistic. It's essentially as if one were to take a player's Batting Average and then add their Fielding Percentage to that and then declare it to be some sort of WAR-derivative, total-value metric.

10-year-old Dean is about to get angry at me, but let's talk math for just one second. In an effort to add two fractions, those fractions are required to share what? Anyone? Hello?

Bueller? Bueller?

That's right, a common denominator! Gold star for you! What that means in baseball terms is that both OBP and SLG have to share a common number by which both total bases (for slugging) and H+BB+HBP (for OBP) are divided, and that is, as you may know, not the case with those particular statistics.

The formula for OBP is the total of a player's hits, BB and HBP divided by that player's total Plate Appearances. SLG percentage is a player's total bases divided by at-bats. In other words:

$$OBP = (H + BB + HBP) / Plate\ Appearances$$
$$SLG = (1B + 2*2B + 3*3B + 4*HR) / At\text{-}Bats$$

So, if a player reaches bases 244 times in 723 PA, and a player amasses 329 total bases in 651 AB, you would be adding 244/723 and 329/651, which you can't actually do. When you simplify the fractions of OBP and SLG to have a common denominator, sometimes the fractions end up with numbers as high 400,000 before you can find any common denominators. And once you do that, the actual value of a player's OPS may be slightly different. For instance, in the example I just gave, a player who had those ratios for OBP and SLG would have had an OBP of .337 and a SLG of .505, making his OPS .842. However, if you properly add the fractions, the simplest fraction works out to 6,297/7,471, and the true OPS is found to be .843. I know it's a small difference, but the fact that OPS is not fully mathematically sound poses a serious issue. But that's not all.

To give another example of the holes in OPS, in 2017, Matt Carpenter of the St. Louis Cardinals had an OPS of .835, which was 50th in all of baseball. His OBP was .384 and his SLG was .451, which were 17th and 79th, respectively. His OPS, by rounding to the thousandths place, is tied with Mike Moustakas of the Kansas City Royals during the 2017 season (he was traded to Milwaukee at the deadline in 2018). By OPS' standards, the two players should have essentially identical production, right? Wrong.

Player	*Avg.*	*OBP*	*SLG*	*OPS*	*wOBA*	*wRC+*	*Off. RAA*
Carpenter	.241	.384	.451	*.835*	.361	123	18.9
Moustakas	.272	.314	.521	*.835*	.345	114	4.7

To explain some of these statistics, wRC+, or weighted runs created plus, is a metric where a player's offensive production is determined based on wOBA and park effects, essentially leveling the playing field so guys in more hitter-friendly parks don't have an unfair advantage. 100 is average and every point above 100 is 1% above league average. Offensive RAA is runs above average, strictly on the offensive side of the baseball, taking batting and base running into account, among other things.

As you can see, despite the OPS being identical, the numbers tell two different stories. Depending on how you look at it, Moustakas had a higher Batting Average and SLG, but Carpenter got on base more far more, walking 45 more times than Moustakas. In addition, Carpenter produced better in all the advanced metrics than Moustakas did. Combining that with his higher OBP, many would argue that his overall offensive production was superior to that of Moustakas.

Moustakas got more hits and tallied more total bases than Carpenter, so from a traditional statistical standpoint, his year appears to have been more productive. On the other hand, Carpenter walked far more, despite getting less hits and having less AB, which accounts for the higher wOBA and wRC+. So, depending on how you choose to evaluate a hitter, one of them had a better 2017 season than the other no matter how you look at it, unless you use OPS as your go-to measuring stick.

Carpenter's ability to reach base safely at a higher rate and have a significantly better BB/K ratio than Moustakas (Carpenter had 109 BB/125 K, Moustakas had 34 BB/94 K) is likely a large contributor to what allowed Carpenter to come out on top in terms of overall production. However, their OPS were still the same, despite a noticeable difference in other statistics. If, from a traditional standpoint, Moustakas looked better, and from an advanced perspective, Carpenter looked better, how are their OPS totals the same? It just continues to show that OPS is not reliable in terms of assessing production, because based on OPS, two seemingly identical players are shown to be anything but in just about any other offensive category.

It's a nice thought, but mathematically it can be inaccurate and tedious to accurately calculate, and at the end of the day it doesn't actually measure any one thing. It's more of a mash-up of important statistics passed off as some sort of deeper look into the total production of a hitter. I'm all for all-encompassing statistics in baseball, ones that tell the whole story, however OPS is not one of them, and struggles with the basic concepts of math. Many of the analytical minds out there that swear up and down that projecting and measuring baseball production is simply math and raw data should understand and agree that there is a serious issue with a statistic that isn't even mathematically sound. In my opinion, a more effective version of OPS would be some sort of adjusted OPS or "true" OPS. Let's call it True OPS for now. For the record, this is completely made up and is just a thought I've been having regarding OPS and its shortcomings. Essentially the difference would be doing the long version of adding OBP and SLG, adjusting for some of the potentially miscalculated totals that exist in the current edition of OPS.

What True OPS is in relation to OPS is simply a correction of the OPS ratios that turn out to be incorrect. The example I provided at the opening of the chapter would be an example of an incorrect OPS calculation and one that would be reflected in True OPS. His OPS would be .842 and his True OPS would be .843. It doesn't seem like a big difference, and maybe it isn't, but any difference trending in the right direction is worthwhile in my opinion, especially when it is righting a mathematical wrong.

In the top 50 OPS totals from the 2017 season, there were six instances in which the OPS listed did not match the OPS that was found when properly adding the two fractions (H+BB+HBP/AB+BB+HBP+SF and

Total Bases/AB). If you expand that to the 750 players in Major League Baseball at any given time, you'd have approximately 90 players whose OPS will be improperly calculated, and produce an incorrect total.

Usually, the difference is only one or two points, but the fact that the statistic is wrong in the first place is sufficient enough a problem to warrant a conversation about either adjusting OPS or finding a different way to assess the value of a hitter. After all, even when we fix the math, OPS doesn't really calculate any one thing, and the two things it does calculate are unrelated in execution, which leads me to my next point.

Another option would be to incorporate some variation of OPS, something like BAPS, or Batting Average Plus Slugging, which would essentially just add Batting Average and SLG together where OPS adds OBP and SLG. I believe that this would be more effective because, firstly, it would eliminate some of the clutter surrounding OPS. OPS takes walks, hit by pitches and sacrifice flies in addition to hits and types of hits into account when being calculated, where BAPS would simply be frequency of hits and types of hits. Not to mention the fact that Batting Average and SLG are both divided by AB, making it a lot easier (and more accurate) to calculate.

Not to mention, BAPS is more fun to say. C'mon, say it! *Baps. Baaps. Baaaaaaps.* It's more enjoyable to say a word than read an acronym, in my opinion.

OPS has the right idea, it's just impractical to execute, given the "simplicity" with which it's presented. It's also cluttered in terms of how much information it's trying to sort and present in a coherent manner. Hits, walks and hit by pitches in PA in addition to consistency of extra base hits per AB sits on the neatness spectrum somewhere between a flea market and a broken piñata at a children's party. Hits plus extra-base hits is a little cleaner and a little more area-specific.

If we can bring back the Matt Carpenter and Mike Moustakas example for just a moment, we can see how BAPS differentiates between what it measures accurately, where OPS does not necessarily accomplish that same task. OPS can have two players who are completely different in almost every way imaginable and have their OPS be exactly the same. Matt Carpenter seemed to fare better in the advanced metrics, where Moustakas had better numbers by percentages. BAPS, at least in the world of percentage-based statistics, is accurate in quantifying both how frequently a player gets a hit and how much power they can be expected to hit for when they do get a hit.

Without further ado, here is the very first BAPS chart:

Player	BA	SLG	BAPS
Matt Carpenter	.241	.451	**.692**
Mike Moustakas	.272	.521	**.793**

Moustakas had a better Batting Average and a better Slugging Percentage, so naturally his BAPS is better, as opposed to OPS where Matt Carpenter had a better OBP and lower SLG and Moustakas had higher SLG and lower OBP, yet both numbers were the same. Moustakas totaled more hits and more total bases and BAPS indicates that. OPS, as we've seen, does not.

I think the best measurement of how accurate or the quality of measurement that a statistic or metric provides is to see the correlation between that statistic or metric and some other valuable metrics. If I could, I'd like to take several of the most well-known metrics and assess the correlation between them and BAPS, OPS and True OPS, respectively.

Metric	Correlation To (*r* value):			
	Off. RAA	oWAR	wRC+	wOBA
BAPS	.832	.744	.824	.895
OPS	.870	.749	.904	.984
True OPS	.871	.750	.905	.984

Again, Off. RAA is Offensive Runs Above Average, and is essentially the same as WAR, except it is calculated in runs instead of wins. It takes into account a player's offensive game only, including batting and base running in its calculation. oWAR is offensive WAR, which accounts for how many wins above replacement-level a player's offensive game provides his team.

Again, if I may get mathematical with you for just a moment: In calculating a linear relationship between two categories (linear meaning as one value increase or decreases, the other increases or decreases at the same rate), one can determine how linear a relationship is by finding the correlation coefficient, or the r value. An r value that is closer to 1.0 is more linear, where an r value closer to 0.0 shows a less linear correlation.

As you can see, with the exception of wRC+, all three metrics generally have a strong correlation to the stat they're being compared to. Generally, an r value between .800 and 1.000 is considered "strong," while somewhere in the .600-.800 range would be considered "medium." The main thing I'd like you to notice from this graphic is that our new True OPS has a stronger relationship than OPS in all four categories. Granted, it's only .001 stronger across the board with the exception of wOBA, for which it is .0001 greater (.9843 to .9482), but by simply adjusting the calculation of OPS so that it's mathematically accurate, there is a tangible and measurable increase in the strength of correlation between it and Off. RAA, Offensive WAR (oWAR) and wRC+, even if it is a minute one.

I would also like to point out that BAPS is noticeably the least linear in all four categories. I assume this is in large part because most of these metrics are designed to incorporate the aspects of OPS, and BAPS measures something quite different, potentially causing the correlations to be less strong than in the case of OPS and True OPS. Either way, as I said, I'm not in this to sell new creations of mine, I'm simply exploring the possibilities of statistics that are more coherent and more sound mathematically than OPS. BAPS may not relate as strongly to some of these metrics, but I assert that it still may hold some value, depending on what you hold dear. If it's being able to measure two like statistics and do so in a mathematically sound way, then BAPS may hold some value, although it is different than OPS and True OPS.

True OPS, on the other hand, is more linear than OPS. True OPS, as we know, is the exact same as OPS, the only difference being we adjust some of the mathematically inaccurate calculations of OPS. It's a small adjustment, but any movement toward a completely linear correlation is a positive one and one that should willingly be made by those in pursuit of the "perfect" metrics. And if simply correcting the math on OPS makes the correlation more linear, I believe it's time to either change the way we calculate OPS or move on from it altogether in favor of something else. I'm neither for nor opposed to either option, I simply want to make the numbers make sense and be mathematically accurate to what they claim to measure.

The fact of the matter is that OPS is liable to have the occasional miscalculation which can lead to a player's OPS being incorrect. For some reason, if a player's OPS was listed at .999 but, when calculated correctly, actually came out to be 1.000, and that was the difference in an MVP voting, that would be a travesty and an embarrassment to the folks who swear by math and crunching numbers in evaluating players. We have seen this to be possible, and the possibility of up to 100 or more instances of this taking place across Major League rosters during any given season should be enough to encourage us as a community to more closely examine OPS and potentially gravitate toward a more consistently accurate measurement in True OPS.

As I said, True OPS is, at the most, *slightly* more reliable than OPS, if at all, in terms of overall distribution and its value as a mathematically sound figure. I know it's only slight, but it's better than nothing. At the end of the day, OPS still contains the possibility of a mathematical inaccuracy skewing the numbers, which does not exist in True OPS. Those things, in itself, show that an adjustment needs to be made in OPS. We cannot be selling numbers that could potentially be wrong. Not for all the strict allegiance to the Math Gods that takes place in front offices these days (Maybe *Math Gods vs. Baseball Gods: The Holy War* would have been a good title. I'll keep that in mind for the movie adaptation).

Quick disclaimer before we move on: I'm not claiming BAPS or True OPS as real things or attempting to sell these new metrics I've created, nor am I submitting them to Baseball Prospectus for validation, I'm just asking you to think about it. Think about the holes in OPS' game and see how other options would better educate the fans and more clearly illustrate a player's offensive production.

Traditional Conclusion

T raditional statistics have their place in baseball, given they do their job and can accurately demonstrate a player's worth and ability to produce on the field. Some of them do a better job than others of course, and I wouldn't be doing a good job of presenting fair and unbiased points if I didn't acknowledge that. However, I do believe that there are benefits to a lot of the statistics that have been labeled "outdated," "obsolete" or from the tongue of harsher critics, "stupid."

These measures have been present in our game for as long as the dirt that marks its fiercest warriors and is as much engrained in its DNA as hot dogs, apple pie and Chevrolet. Again, to say they're all awesome and need to be a part of the analytical process would be overstating things, but for the most part, they do their job. Nothing more, nothing less.

Batting Average will always be a staple in the game. So many of the most memorable moments in the sports' history have come by way of the hit. Kirk Gibson's 1988 World Series HR. David Freese's two-strike, two-out triple in the ninth inning, allowing the St. Louis Cardinals to come back and win Game Six of the 2011 World Series, leading to a Game Seven and Series win. Luis Gonzalez hitting a walk-off single in Game Seven of the 2001 World Series, preventing the Yankees' four-peat. All hits. Hank Aaron passing Babe Ruth with his 715th career HR, Joe Carter with a walk-off HR in Game Six to win the World Series for the Blue Jays. The game revolves around hits, it always has and it always will. If hits are important, and getting them consistently is important, why isn't the only statistic out there that specifically measures the frequency with which players are getting hits given more respect? It does its job and that's all you can ask. Hits are still as important as ever, arguably more so, so it would seem the game hasn't really changed *that* much.

Bunting, and small ball in general is not nearly as ineffective as people try to make it out to be. There is absolutely a place for it in the game, and some of the most successful managers in baseball's history have relied on it to win multiple World Series like Tony LaRussa or long-time manager Billy Martin, founder of "Billy Ball."

Billy Ball was a hyper-aggressive style of play that was seen in teams managed by Billy Martin in the 1980s. It included, but was not limited to, a high volume of stolen base attempts and bunts to go along with soaring pitch counts, which will undoubtedly cause a chill to run down the spine of modern pitching coaches. Overall, it was a brash style of play, but it saw results.

Rickey Henderson was a primary beneficiary of Billy Ball, recording 100 SB in his first full season, and we all know how his career on the base paths turned out. Martin's teams saw their share of success as well. Martin's teams won five division titles, two American League championships and one World Series championship in 16 seasons of Martin's managerial tenure. Tony LaRussa also saw a lot of hardware, winning six pennants (three in the American League and three in the National League) and three World Series titles in 33 seasons at the helm of a Major League team. I'm not saying small ball is the only way, but the proof is in the pudding: it's definitely one of the ways.

Granted, bunting and stealing wildly will cause more harm than good, but if one can do it efficiently, why would you not use all the tools at your disposal to win? These things were created and utilized for so long for a reason. While some may not agree, I don't personally believe it's wise to completely discredit something and eliminate it entirely.

Of course, that logic only stands if the statistic or strategy makes sense.

Pitching wins are a nice way to see how good a pitcher's team is, but is not able, on its own, to give an accurate view of a pitcher's performance. OPS is simply a shortcut through math in an attempt to produce a wide-view statistic that doesn't necessarily indicate production in any one facet of the offensive game. These may have their place too, but that place probably shouldn't be in the "elevator pitch" version of a player's statistical breakdown or on the short list that shows up on the back of a guy's baseball card.

In a lot of areas, I consider myself more traditional than progressive. Baseball is not necessarily an exception. However, as a coach, it's not my job to stick to my guns in terms of theory. My job is to know about everything out there and utilize what I find is useful. It doesn't matter if something became popular in 1895 or 2018, it's my obligation as someone who considers himself a "baseball man" to accept all information until I feel it can't help me, and it is your responsibility as well if you consider yourself the same.

There is no conceivable reason to brush off any new information about the game simply because you "don't like the looks of it." Just because it may be coming from an algorithm developed by a 24-year old MBA instead of a grizzled, 70-year old lifer doesn't mean it's any less applicable (it also doesn't mean it's any better, but that's for another section). The point is that information is information, and if any of it can help you as a player, coach, front office executive, scout or any of the other monumentally important people that work so hard to continue creating a successful baseball program or organization, why wouldn't you at least give it a look? To me, it's one of two reasons:

1.) You're a walking supercomputer, or
2.) You're more interested in being right than being correct.

And there is a difference.

To me, being right means whatever you say, goes. Being correct means that what you're saying holds water, it can be tried and tested and will be proven to be accurate to how you presented it. The issue with being correct is, often times, to get there means you were wrong somewhere along the way and nobody likes to be wrong, especially in an argument the size of the one going on from one end of the baseball spectrum to the other. But, somebody's got to do it if we want to get anywhere on this issue as a baseball community.

So, while fond of many traditional ideas and practices present in the game of baseball, I also understand that there are many benefits – and drawbacks – of the new sabermetric-driven, analytical movement taking place in baseball today.

PART 3

The Benefits Of Sabermetrics

I must admit, a few years ago I never would have believed I'd be using "sabermetrics" and "benefit" in the same sentence. I can hear a younger version of myself cussing me under his breath. However, that was then and this is now, and here we are! I have been convinced that, to a certain extent, the sabermetric community may be on to something. If any of you data-heads made it through the first two parts of this book, then your door prize for part three is to hear me say nice things about sabermetrics.

I used to be very skeptical, and I have no issue admitting that in some areas I still am. I struggle to accept statistics or measurements that I can't do on my own with a calculator. I also struggle to accept metrics that have names that contain both lower and uppercase letters, numbers and symbols all in one, it just seems, I don't know, yucky. Strikes me as more fitting for a bank account password than a baseball statistic. However, in my old age (I'm 26 years old as of the publishing of this book), I've mellowed out some and have come to understand that just because I don't completely understand it *yet*, doesn't mean it's not viable. A lesson a lot of people could stand to benefit from learning, but I'm not here to preach!

The sabermetric community has done a good job of taking some of the most minute details and intricacies of play and applying them into statistics that tell a story. Things like expected run values, linear weights, park effects and other things that may not even occur to the average fan are now at their fingertips. The issue with that is that baseball people love, and I mean *love*, statistics, so the cooler the presentation, the more likely people are to accept these stats as gospel.

So, at the risk of people accepting statistics because their names sound way cooler than traditional statistics (looking at you, wOBA), I am going to lay out some of the benefits as well as potential limitations or shortcomings of the sabermetric movement. While it's new and fun just like that car you just bought, if something is snarled under the hood, it's going to blow up in your face. I'm no mechanic, but let's take a look and see what we can find.

Chapter 6
Let's End the War on WAR

F resh-out-of-college Dean is *so* mad at me right now. What does he know? He's a child.

WAR, or Wins Above Replacement is the closest anyone in base-ball has come to quantifying a player's total contribution. It takes into account batting, defense, pitching, base running, park effects (leveling the playing field because some parks are hitters' parks and some are pitchers' parks), and more to give you one number to encapsulate a player's total value. Let's take a slightly deeper look at WAR before I start explaining why it's useful.

The nature of WAR is pretty self-explanatory. It shows how many additional wins a player adds or costs his team in comparison to a "replacement" level player. Generally, the replacement level player is viewed as a Triple-A player just called up to the Major Leagues.

For some context, the highest single-season WAR ever was Babe Ruth's 1923 season, in which his WAR was 15.0, meaning had a brand new big league player taken all of Babe Ruth's AB and defensive innings in 1923, the Yankees would have lost 15 more games than they did with Ruth in the lineup. For reference, Ruth slashed .393/.545/.764 in 1923. He also ended the season with 41 HR and 130 RBI, both of which were the highest total in the league that season (only one other player exceeded 20 HR, and Ruth was one of only five players to eclipse 100 RBI). The lowest single-season WAR ever was in 1933, by Jim Levey of the then-St. Louis Browns (now Baltimore Orioles), with a -4.0 WAR, meaning that the Browns would have won four more games had they had a league average player instead of Levey. In 1933, Levey slashed .195/.237/.240 with two HR and 36 RBI in 141 games.

Generally, the league leader in WAR ends up somewhere between 7.0 and 10.0. FanGraphs provides this chart to better break down how WAR totals stack up:

Designation	WAR
Scrub	0-1
Role Player	1-2
Solid Starter	2-3
Good Player	3-4
All-Star	4-5
Superstar	5-6
MVP	6+

To paint you a better picture, in 2017, the two league MVPs, Miami's Giancarlo Stanton and Houston's Jose Altuve totaled a 7.3 and 7.6 WAR, respectively. In Mike Trout's two MVP seasons (2014 and 2016), his WAR totals were 8.3 and 9.6[8]. To put it plainly, over six is great, over eight will *almost* always result in an MVP (sorry, 2017 Aaron Judge), and over 10 is a historically great season. A lot of people haven't bought in on WAR yet, and I think those people will ultimately be left behind. WAR, as previously mentioned, is really the only statistic that takes every facet of a player's game into account, as well as adjusts numbers for ballpark effects amongst other things, allowing players of different seasons and eras to be compared relatively, if you're into that kind of thing. It also generally places an equal weight on all measures. Let's take a look at the position players and pitchers who finished top-five in WAR in 2017 and see how the numbers stack up.

---

[8] WAR data via FanGraphs

Player	WAR	OBP Rank	SLG Rank	wOBA Rank	wRC+ Rank	DRS Rank	UZR Rank
Judge	8.2	3	3	2	2	13	13
Altuve	7.6	6	16	7	4	6	9
Stanton	7.3	22	1	5	5	9	10
Trout	6.9	2	2	1	1	44	46
Rendon	6.7	9	21	14	13	6	1

Just for a refresher, wOBA is weighted On-Base Average, which applies linear weights to outcomes such as BB, HBP, and each type of hit to essentially provide a more exact version of Slugging Percentage. wRC+ is, again, Weighted Runs Created Plus, which assesses a player's total offensive production by illustrating how many runs above league average they are. If 100 is league average, then every point above or below 100 is 1% better or worse than league average (i.e., wRC+ of 120 is 20% better than league average). However, you may be asking yourself, "What in the world is 'DRS' and 'UZR'?" Allow me to elaborate.

DRS stands for Defensive Runs Saved, and it is essentially a description of how many defensive runs a player contributes to or costs his team relative to an exactly league average player. It takes into account a wide variety of other defensive metrics to come to a number of total runs saved. FanGraphs provides a chart for reference as to what constitutes a good, or bad, DRS total:

Defensive Rating	DRS
Gold Glove Caliber	15+
Great	10
Above Average	5
Average	0
Below Average	-5
Poor	-10
Awful	-15

As for UZR, it is a similar metric but is calculated differently. UZR can be read and interpreted exactly the same as the DRS chart previously shown, however, it is found through different means. UZR takes range and arm strength more into account than DRS, causing UZR to be more a measure of a player's *potential* or ability to save runs, where DRS is a measure of how many runs they *actually* saved compared to league average, at least that's way I've come to interpret the difference. Again, expected runs vs. actual runs, so whatever your cup of tea, feel free to apply as you wish. Either way, both of them are very popular metrics used to calculate defensive ability.

Now, let's get back into the numbers, shall we?

As you can see in the visual a page or so back, the top five position player WAR totals in 2017 all rank very highly in many of the main statistical categories, both offensive and defensive.

For Aaron Judge, he was elite offensively in 2017, finishing in the top three in OBP, SLG, wOBA, wRC+ and had a slash line of .284/.422/.627. His 52 HR were second in MLB behind Giancarlo Stanton's 59, and was MVP runner-up behind Houston's Jose Altuve, who happened to be second in WAR in 2017. His elite offensive numbers are supplemented by the fact that he is also an upper-echelon defender among outfielders. Keep in mind there are three every day outfielders on 30 MLB teams, so essentially out of 90+ outfielders that play every day, Aaron Judge ranked 13th in both of the major defensive metrics, DRS and UZR. However, there are also instances where players weren't consistently great across the board, yet still finished high on the final leaderboard. Flaw in WAR, or simply being great in one facet outweighing being less-than-great in the other?

Mike Trout, the WAR darling and, in my opinion, the best player in baseball by a wide margin (he's also from New Jersey, so, bonus points), had an interesting 2017 season in terms of overall production. As always, he put up huge numbers, ranking either first or second in OBP, SLG, wOBA and wRC+, however he was fourth in the league in WAR. One needs to simply look at his defensive metrics for an explanation.

Trout's DRS and UZR are both exceptionally average. If you take the same approximately 90 every day outfielders in the MLB, Trout's 44th-ranked DRS and 46th-ranked UZR are perfectly middle of the pack. Personally, I don't see how he ranks so low on the defensive metrics. I know he doesn't have Jackie Bradley Jr.'s 100-mph Howitzer right arm, but he is among the speediest players in the league, despite being built like a Middle Linebacker, which would indicate good range and has been responsible for more than a handful of memorable HR robberies over the years which would confirm it. However, I didn't watch every single game he played during the 2017 season, so I can't say for sure.

Either way, the fact that Trout was elite offensively and pedestrian flashing the leather both contributed to Trout falling behind three players, only one of whom finished ahead of him in even a single offensive category (Stanton had a higher SLG). However, the numbers can have the opposite effect on a player's WAR. Enter: Anthony Rendon.

Rendon is the enigmatic, albeit extremely talented third baseman for the Washington Nationals. He shows flashes of being one of the most talented players in baseball, yet often slides under the radar, most likely due to the astronomical fame of some of his teammates: Bryce Harper, Max Scherzer and Steven Strasburg, to name a few. He has yet to have shown himself to be a consistently dominant player with the bat, however he usually hits in the middle of a very talented Washington lineup and has done nothing but carry his weight. While he is a very productive offensive player, I would hesitate to classify him as a juggernaut swinging the bat, with the likes of a Mike Trout or other players in that altitude. Even with his offensive prowess being as high-quality as it is, his glove is still likely what adds a large portion of his overall value.

Among MLB 3B, Rendon ranks sixth in DRS and first in UZR. Essentially, he is a top-five defensive third baseman and combining that with him being an above-average, but not necessarily among the *absolute* best, offensive player (ninth in OBP, 21st in SLG, 14th in wOBA and 13th in wRC+), allowed him to tally 2017's fifth-best WAR total, with 6.7.

WAR does a good job of illustrating a player's overall contributions. There is a lot that goes into it, so it is definitely messy at times to decipher and figure out what went into a player's total. One of my main knocks against WAR is that it's not really an *observable* statistic. In other words, I could go to a game, watch a player go 1-4 and say, "His batting average is .250." However, I couldn't go to a game and say, "He had a 0.2 WAR game," unless I had two graphing calculators, an abacus, 13 pencil erasers and my very own MIT grad in tow. It's tough to see *why* a player's WAR is the way it is. However, that doesn't change that it, at the end of the day, truly is the way it is. WAR is confusing, but the number that is ultimately produced is legit. For further evidence, if you take a look at many former Most Valuable Player recipients and Cy Young winners, you'll see WAR's consistency and accuracy in determining whose seasons were truly the most productive.

Below is a chart displaying the last 10 seasons' worth of MVP awards and the recipients' overall rank in WAR.

MVP				
Season	*League*	*WAR Rank*	*League*	*WAR Rank*
2017	AL	3	NL	5
2016	AL	1	NL	3
2015	AL	3	NL	1
2014	AL	1	NL	2
2013	AL	2	NL	3
2012	AL	5	NL	2
2011	AL	14	NL	9
2010	AL	1	NL	5
2009	AL	7	NL	3
2008	AL	15	NL	1

According to FanGraphs, in the last 10 seasons (2008-2017), out of the 20 league Most Valuable Player awards (MVPs), 10 for National League and 10 for American League, only seven of them had a season that didn't finish in the top three in all of Major League Baseball in WAR. In four of those seasons, the three players with the highest WAR totals for the season all either finished as a league MVP or an MVP runner-up. This evidence clearly demonstrates WAR's accuracy in assessing a player's production.

In the past, the Baseball Writers' Association of America (BBWAA, the organization that votes on post-season awards, Hall of Fame induction, etc.) and the sabermetrics community butted heads like a couple of Bighorn Sheep. However, the last few years have been an indication that, whether they know it or not, their voting has lined up pretty closely with final WAR totals. Again, whether or not that is a conscious decision by writers to take WAR into account is something that you'll have to ask each individual voter, however based on some pieces like Bob Ryan's 2013, "WAR Stat in Baseball is Complete Nonsense," the jury may still be out on how some of the seasoned writers and, in turn, voters for baseball's major awards feel about WAR. The rub is, even if they don't like it, often times their vote for best player is also the guy with one of the three highest WAR totals for that season! Imagine the dumbfounded look on someone's face when they spend a season bashing WAR only to find their vote for MVP had the highest WAR total in the league. Comical! However, the head-spinning won't end there: The correlations continue when you look at Cy Young voting.

Cy Young is an award given to the pitcher who is deemed to have had the best season on the mound. Again, like MVP, there is a Cy Young given to a pitcher in both in American League and National League. So, if we take the same time frame (2008-2017) and look at the 20 Cy Youngs given out during that time, we see WAR's correlation with top pitcher performances as well.

Cy Young				
Season	*Lg.*	*Pitcher WAR Rank* [9]	*Lg.*	*Pitcher WAR Rank*
2017	AL	2	NL	3
2016	AL	6	NL	3
2015	AL	6	NL	2
2014	AL	2	NL	1
2013	AL	4	NL	1
2012	AL	4	NL	6
2011	AL	4	NL	2
2010	AL	4	NL	3
2009	AL	1	NL	3
2008	AL	4	NL	2

Remember: all of these rankings were those of pitchers who won the Cy Young award in their respective season. If you look at the chart, you'll see that there are only three instances out of the 20 total awards where the Cy Young winner was not a top-five finisher in Pitcher WAR. And while there are a lot of other metrics by which people analyze pitchers other than WAR (Wins, ERA, IP, K, FIP, ERA+, etc.), you can see that WAR, in the end, lines up with the best in the game far more often than not. There are actually no instances in the last 10 years when a Cy Young award winner has finished outside the top 10 in pitcher WAR for that season. That happed twice in MVP voting (2011, Justin Verlander and 2008, Dustin Pedroia). Although, in 2011 Verlander's overall WAR being outside the top 10 is most likely due to the fact that he is a pitcher.

Generally speaking, pitchers have lower WAR totals than position players. They play in less games over the course of the year, and often times leave the game early, being pulled for a reliever before the conclusion of nine innings. I always figured this was the main reason you rarely find pitchers in the top five of any single season's WAR rankings, unless they were having a historically dominant year. Due to this,

---

[9] WAR data via FanGraphs

pitchers have their own category of WAR called pitcher WAR, which applies a more uniform model to keep all pitchers on a level plane and separate from position players. Justin Verlander was fourth in Major League Baseball in pitcher WAR in 2011.

Those who oppose WAR will often say things to the effect that it's based on a judgment, and that this magical "replacement player" doesn't exist. I'd agree with that. However, one can't argue with the general accuracy with which WAR indicates the players that had the best season any given year, offensively or on the mound, so much so that sometimes even those that dispute WAR's validity end up being in agreement with its final totals. Sometimes there are anomalies, like in the American League voting in 2011 and 2008. This is most likely due to the fact that some voters value certain things over others. For example, in 2011, as we discussed, Justin Verlander was fourth in pitcher WAR but finished 14th overall in WAR. He had a record of 24-5, 2.40 ERA and had 250 K in 251 IP, among other things. He led the league in Wins, Games Started, ERA, IP and K. Was he the most valuable to his team overall? Possibly not. However, his pitching season was so dominant that they ended up giving him the award. I am personally not a fan of pitchers winning the MVP, mainly because I think position players play every day and that in itself makes a dominant position player season more valuable than a pitcher's season. A pitcher could be sensational and single-handedly carry a team to victory every start, and the team could still, in theory, only win 33 or 34 games. Besides, pitchers already have the Cy Young, which is the highest honor in the land of pitchers.

I personally see the shortcomings of WAR, however this section is charged with laying out the benefits to it (I'll get to some of the potential drawbacks later on). In short, it's the only true measure that assesses all of the facets of baseball performance in one. As evidenced by MVP and Cy Young voting over the last 10 seasons, it's also done a quality job of accurately assessing a player's overall value and performance in accordance with the way the voters evaluate players. At the end of the day, every statistic and metric alike is trying to do the same thing: evaluate baseball players. WAR is a way to do that and to convey value based on a "league average" player, albeit an imaginary one. Although, in theory you could compare the desired player to a player with a 0.0 WAR player if you wanted a measuring stick with a pulse.

Ultimately, WAR doesn't need war declared on it. It simply needs to be better understood. It's a versatile metric, which uses *a lot* of data in its calculation. So at the very least, that effort and that amount of unique data collection and application should be rewarded by giving it a shot. It's daunting on the surface, I was guilty of it as well. I would go on rants about how WAR doesn't make sense, and that WAR supporters are trying to change the game, or are fascist, or something along those lines. Tough to recall, you see, as it was a few years ago. Either way, I've done the necessary research, I've seen the type of players that lead in WAR and how my then-strictly traditional views unknowingly supported the findings of WAR. With that, I eventually came to the conclusion that, generally speaking, WAR describes in one number and a tenths-place decimal what it would take a slash line (Batting Average/OBP/SLG), SB and SB success rate, several defensive statistics and possibly more to encompass, and it does so with marked accuracy in terms of what the other numbers say to supplement. Just because it's confusing and algorithm-driven doesn't mean it's bad. It just means it's confusing and algorithm-driven. Call off the dogs and hold your fire in the face of WAR. It means well and does well.

Chapter 7
WHOA-ba: How wOBA
has Surpassed SLG

W OBA. It's fun to say. It reminds me of the sound in a cartoon when a fat man is walking down the street.

Wo-ba, wo-ba, wo-ba.

No! This is serious, wOBA is serious! Sorry, I can sometimes get lost down a rabbit hole brought about by the most random thoughts… What were we talking about again?

Right, wOBA. wOBA, or weighted On-Base Average, is a linear weights metric used to determine a player's overall batting production. This is not a metric like WAR that takes various aspects of a player's game into account. wOBA simply determines the damage a hitter does with a bat in his hands.

wOBA assigns a weight to BB, HBP, sometimes reached on error (depending on the calculation), 1B, 2B, 3B and HR. The weight is based on overall run expectancy of each outcome. We've seen the formula for wOBA earlier in this book, but to refresh your memory for this section:

$$wOBA = \frac{.69 \times uBB + .72 \times HBP + .89 \times 1B + 1.27 \times 2B + 1.62 \times 3B + 2.10 \times HR}{AB + BB - IBB + SF + HBP}$$

So, based on FanGraphs' formula (above), a .69 run weight is placed on a BB, .72 runs on HBP and so on. The total run value of all the player's outcomes is then divided by plate appearances, of course excluding intentional BB, because a player doesn't technically earn that directly through any actions of his own.

Much like WAR, wOBA is a very accurate indication of how productive a player's season is, both on the field and in the eyes of the "powers that be," or the BBWAA. Again, a lot of writers have been known to be anti-sabermetrics, although many have come around as of late. Let's take a look at the last 10 seasons' leaders in wOBA and see how they fared in the post-season awards voting.

[10]

Season	*wOBA Leader*	*wOBA*	*SLG*	*Off. RAA*	*Awards*
2017	Mike Trout	.437*	.629*	54.9	MVP – 4th
2016	David Ortiz	.419*	.620*	37.5	MVP – 6th
2015	Bryce Harper	.461*	.649*	77.7*	**MVP**
2014	A. McCutchen	.412*	.542	51.3	MVP – 3rd
2013	Miguel Cabrera	.455*	.636*	62.6	**MVP**
2012	Miguel Cabrera	.417*	.606*	46.2	**MVP**
2011	José Bautista	.443*	.608*	66.3*	MVP – 3rd
2010	Josh Hamilton	.445*	.633*	55.3	**MVP**
2009	Albert Pujols	.447*	.658*	70.5*	**MVP**
2008	Albert Pujols	.459*	.653*	67.7*	**MVP**

*league leader

It's evident that wOBA's correlation with MVP awards is similarly accurate to that of WAR, if not even more so. Of the last 10 seasons' wOBA leaders, six of them have gone on to win the MVP of their respective league. In addition, two others were MVP finalists (top three vote-getters). So, in the last 10 seasons, the league leader in wOBA was an MVP finalist 80% of the time, winning the award 60% of the time. However, one of the numbers on the chart above seems to not fit with the rest. How did Andrew McCutchen lead the league in wOBA despite having a Slugging Percentage over 100 points less than some of the others on the list? The answer is why wOBA is an effective metric in evaluating players.

---

[10] wOBA, Off. RAA data via FanGraphs, SLG/MVP results via Baseball Reference

McCutchen's slash line during his season in 2014 was .314/.410/.542. He had 25 HR and 83 RBI, though he did tie his career high in doubles that season with 38. McCutchen's .410 OBP led the league, which would have landed him outside of the league's top five finishers in most other seasons from 2008-2017. However, in 2014, it was the best in the league, and that's how he also led the league in wOBA. He hit a lot, sure, but he also got on base more than anyone else and wOBA values getting on base proportionately as opposed to statistics like SLG or OBP by itself.

McCutchen got a lot of hits, batting .314 in 2014. However, he didn't hit for exceptional power compared to other names on the list of wOBA leaders. As we saw, his SLG was .542, which was actually sixth best in baseball that season. He hit 38 doubles, six triples and 25 HR, which means of his 172 hits, 103 of them were singles, which shakes out to be approximately 60% singles. Of the other players on our list, only two players had seasons in which a higher percentage of their hit totals were singles. Those two were Miguel Cabrera in 2013 (63% of 193 hits, he hit .348 with 26 doubles and 44 HR that year) and Josh Hamilton in 2010 (60% of 186 hits, he hit .359 with 40 doubles and 32 HR). Even despite having so many of his hits be singles without hitting for the power numbers of Cabrera and Hamilton, he led the league in wOBA. The answer, again lies in his ability to get on base.

McCutchen walked 84 times in 2014 and was hit by a pitch 10 more, so you can add 94 additional bases to his hit total of 172, which is 266. Divide that by his PA (648), and you get his OBP of .410. That is the only statistical category in which McCutchen led baseball that season. His ranks in other categories:

Category	Total	MLB Rank
OPS	.952	3rd
SLG	.542	6th
2B	38	T-9th
3B	6	T-6th
HR	25	T-12th
BB	84	7th

Despite ranking in the top five in just one of those categories, the fact that McCutchen was consistently in the mix in *all* of them is what allowed him to lead the league in wOBA. As I said, wOBA is a metric that assigns a linear weight to each outcome, meaning that no outcomes are disproportionately weighted higher than the others. So, McCutchen had a very good OPS (even though a very wise man once warned me about the dangers of OPS) and SLG, and he was top 10 in doubles, triples and walks, so each of his relatively high outcomes were assessed appropriately. His total numbers based on the fact that he did everything very well instead of some things great and other things not so well is what caused his wOBA to be as high as it was. His SLG would indicate he was very good, but not the best. His other totals would illustrate, individually, that McCutchen was very good or even elite in some cases, but again, never *the best*, but what about all of those factors combined over the course of a season? That's the true measure of a season, how well all facets of the game are performed. And wOBA is one of the few that offers a good look at that, at least specifically for the offensive side of things.

wOBA takes what SLG tries to do, and simply does it better. Not that SLG isn't without its perks. It's a good model of total bases per AB, which is valuable when identifying power hitters, however it is limited in what it can do beyond that. Slugging essentially weighs a single as one, a double as two, triple as three and a home run as four. Now, a single is worth one base and a home run is worth four, but not all home runs are necessarily four times as valuable as all singles. A two-run single in a one run game in the ninth inning is arguably more valuable than a solo HR in a 10-0 game in the second inning, so not all hits are the same. wOBA does a good job of going deeper into each hit and deriving an expected run-based value to assign to each outcome, and the values change slightly every year, though generally it's only by percentage points. All the years of baseball have set the values in a position where it would take an incredible statistical anomaly in a season to sway them in any significant direction. So for wOBA, all hits are still weighted the same when collecting data, however, every hit of each type has been taken into account to derive the value given to that hit, so it's definitely more rooted in history and fact than SLG, which is simply saying the amount of total bases each hit creates is the value of that hit, which as we know is not always the case.

I will admit that wOBA still has a way to go in properly identifying a way to better show the various types of hits, in other words one-RBI single vs. two-run single, or triple with no one on base vs. a three-run triple. It is evident that not all triples are created the same, and sometimes the average is lower than reality, and sometimes it is higher. Again, in the wOBA formula, a triple, for example, is weighted at 1.62 runs. However, with no one on, that triple results in 0 runs, making that weight 1.62 runs too generous. If a player hits a triple with the bases loaded, that triple is worth three runs, making the weight actually *undervalued* by 1.38 runs. I have toyed with creating a wOBA equivalent that weighs all types of hits individually based on literal run creation. In other words, a single that results in no runs is worth "x," and a single that drives in one run is worth "y," and so on. It would be a much longer formula, and I don't have the access to the information to even workshop it based on past seasons, but the idea would remain the same. That is the one area in which I think wOBA could improve. However, based on the current market, it's one of the best and most in-depth available for its simplicity.

I know the term, "linear weights" makes wOBA sound like some crazy, new-fangled metric that was genetically engineered in a petri dish in some laboratory at SABR (Society for American Baseball Research) headquarters in Phoenix, Arizona, but it's not. It's actually quite harmless once you get to know it. It's a good way to get an overall idea of a player's offensive game. Not just their power, not just their ability to get hits, not just their ability to get on base, but all three, rolled up neatly into one easy to read number. It's accuracy in determining a player's MVP case is irrefutable, and its benefit over Slugging Percentage, among other statistics, is marked. So, while the word "weighted" may be off-putting to those getting long in the tooth as well as the old souls out there, it doesn't change the fact that what wOBA is, is merely Slugging Percentage made more accurate and more all-encompassing. The reluctance to accept WAR and maybe even wRC+ and the like are understandable, I'm not completely sold on all of it myself in some cases. However, wOBA is not one of these that are based on many lengthy algorithms. It's a statistic that I use in my own coaching career to evaluate my players. It literally takes me seconds to calculate it on the spot, or to enter a function into an Excel spreadsheet, and only seconds more than it would take to get a statistic like Slugging Percentage, as it were.

So, no need to fear. wOBA is here! I'm a big fan of wOBA, and it may be the one metric I've taken from the progressive era of baseball and applied it most frequently in my own coaching and evaluating. It does what few others do, and at much less cost of time and effort devoted to calculating, compared to other statistics that boast the same results. wOBA is in fact more accurate and, I can't believe I'm saying this, does what many, if not all, traditional statistics cannot do. And, at least in terms of determining the value of what a player can do while standing in the batter's box, what wOBA *can* do is everything.

Chapter 8
Do it Yourself: FIP, the Good Pitcher on a Bad Team's Best Friend

E very pitcher has dealt with it. You're in a jam, you make a great pitch, and get the batter to hit a weak fly ball. However, your outfielder slips, falls and loses the ball in the lights and it falls in at his feet. It goes as a hit. Two runs score. Earned runs. *Yuck.*

That one play takes your day from 6 IP, 2 ER to 5.2 IP, 4 ER and your game ERA goes from 3.00 to 6.35. Huge shout out to Billy out in left field for dogging it in conditioning drills all offseason. Pitchers on good teams may not understand what I'm saying, but any pitcher who has had a lackluster defense behind him is having a post-traumatic stress reaction and sending out an invite to their support group as we speak. However, there is a pitching metric that can adjust your falsely-inflated ERA and show that your weakly-hit-balls-falling-for-a-hit misfortunes were not yours to own and is a better indication of your individual performance. Introducing: FIP.

FIP, or "Fielding Independent Pitching" is just what it claims to be: a pitching metric that measures a pitching performance independent of any defensive influence. In order to do this, FIP eliminates hits from a pitcher's stat line. It calculates only the outcomes that a pitcher has *complete* control over: Home runs allowed, BB, HBP and K.

You see, these are the only plays during which no defender has anything to do with the play. For a HR, the pitcher makes the pitch and then everyone stands and watches it sail into the fifth row. As for inside-the-park home runs, those are so few and far in between, and despite it generally being due to a defensive miscue, it generally isn't enough to sway the number, though I do recognize that could be a potential snag. As for BB and HBP, it's just the pitcher missing his spots. Sometimes umpires missing calls or a catcher that isn't great at framing pitches come into play, but if you make a pitch and it covers the corner, it's going to be a strike far more often than not, so we're not bailing out pitchers here. Strikeouts, again, are completely in a pitcher's control. So, what FIP does is essentially demonstrate what a pitcher's ERA would be if they experienced exactly average defense and exactly average luck in terms of balls falling in for hits and teams stringing hits together against him.

Why shouldn't a pitcher be penalized for giving up hits?

Generally, he should. However, it is definitely true that hits can be the result of freak occurrences, as was the case in our example at the beginning of the chapter. Also, hits are sometimes left up to the official scorer, which means some hits that go on a pitcher's line are a judgment call by a guy who isn't even down on the field. So, it is possible that earned runs can be skewed, so FIP has tried to eliminate that possibility when displaying a pitcher's performance.

Again, FIP takes HR, BB, HBP and K into account and reads the same as ERA. The formula, according to FanGraphs, is:

$$FIP = \frac{13 \times HR + 3 \times (BB + HBP) - 2 \times K}{IP} + FIP \ constant$$

What is a FIP constant, you ask? The FIP constant is a number that allows FIP to read similarly to ERA. To stay accurate, the FIP constant changes year-by-year. To find the constant for a given season, you essentially just need to find FIP for the league average pitcher (without the addition of a constant) and subtract that from the league average ERA. In other words:

[11] *FIP Constant = lgERA − (((13*lgHR)+(3*(lgBB+lgHBP))−(2*lgK))/lgIP)*

---

[11] FanGraphs

All statistics with "lg" at the beginning is the "league average" of that particular statistic. So, "lgERA" is league average ERA, "lgHR" is league average HR allowed, etc.

Generally speaking, the FIP constant is around 3.10. So, we now understand FIP's function, and we understand how one goes about calculating FIP. So let's take a good look at why it's beneficial and may be a better indicator of current and future performance than ERA.

Let's take a look at the two runners-up for the 2017 Cy Young. They are the Los Angeles Dodgers' Clayton Kershaw in the National League, and Chris Sale of the Boston Red Sox in the American League.

Chris Sale and Clayton Kershaw are two of the very best starting pitchers that Major League Baseball has to offer. Kershaw could likely retire today and be a Hall of Famer, with three Cy Young Awards and a National League MVP to his name. Chris Sale, on the other hand, is less decorated, but extremely effective in own right. In his six full MLB seasons (2012-2017), he has led the league in strikeouts and complete games twice and, conveniently, FIP twice, despite never leading the league in ERA. In addition, despite his three Cy Young Awards, Kershaw has only led the league in FIP twice in his nine full seasons while holding five ERA crowns (2009-2017).

Now, I'm not saying that Chris Sale is better than Clayton Kershaw, because I'm not completely sure I believe that. What I am saying is that it's possible that Kershaw may have been the benefactor of some good luck and good defense, while Sale may have had opposite circumstances. Let's use 2017 as a means to explore.

Below is a chart documenting Kershaw and Sale's pitching statistics from the 2017 season as well as their team's overall DRS and corresponding MLB Rank:

Player	IP	H	BB	K	HR	WHIP	H/9	BB/9	K/9	HR/9	DRS (Rank)
Kershaw	175.0	136	30	202	23	.949	7.0	1.5	10.4	1.2	66 (2nd)
Sale	214.1	165	43	308	24	.970	6.9	1.8	12.9	1.0	69 (1st)

Based on the 2017 statistics, one could infer that Sale had a more productive season than Kershaw. Based on the difference in IP, I adjusted Kershaw's stats as if he pitched 214 innings as Sale did, in an effort to more easily compare:

Player	IP	H	BB	K	HR	WHIP	H/9	BB/9	K/9	HR/9
Kershaw	214	166	37	247	28	.949	7.0	1.5	10.4	1.2
Sale	214.1	165	43	308	24	.970	6.9	1.8	12.9	1.0

So, by rate, Kershaw gave up more hits, more home runs, while collecting less strikeouts than Sale. He would have surrendered fewer walks and allowed fewer base runners overall, but not by a staggering margin. The one statistic I neglected to mention, by design until this point, was ERA. Despite, statistically, having a similar or slightly worse year than Sale, Kershaw finished the season with an ERA of 2.31, while Sale's final ERA was 2.90. Naturally, Kershaw's FIP was also better than Sale's, right?

Wrong.

In 2017, Clayton Kershaw had a FIP of 3.07, which was sixth in baseball, despite his ERA being second, behind only Corey Kluber, who won the American League Cy Young that season (2.25). Sale had a FIP of 2.45, which was tops in the league, despite his 2.90 ERA being sixth in baseball. So how did this happen? The answer may be deeper than just defense.

Both Sale and Kershaw enjoyed pitching with elite defenses behind them in 2017. Sale's Boston Red Sox were first in Major League Baseball in team DRS with 69, while Kershaw's Dodgers were second with 66. So, neither defense was to blame in this scenario and neither pitcher could have seen their ERA be unnecessarily inflated due to poor situational defense. So what exactly happened that caused Chris Sale's ERA to be high while his FIP was low, and why was Kershaw's ERA so low when his FIP was higher? Ready yourselves for the answer none of you want to hear: luck.

One of FIP's aims is to eliminate chance from the assessment of a pitcher's performance. As it appears, since neither pitcher can blame a lackluster defense for their earned run average, sheer luck is to blame for Sale's ERA being where it was. Allow me to explain why.

Again, FIP's measurement is basically what a pitcher's ERA would look like given they experience exactly average defense behind them and exactly average luck in terms of hits falling through and order in which various hits are strung together by opposing offenses. According to his FIP, Chris Sale was the best in the league at controlling what he could control, but saw himself outside the top five looking in when it came time to measure ERA. Clearly, he did not experience poor defensive play behind him, as the Red Sox led Major League Baseball in team Defensive Runs Saved in 2017. So, it would appear that Sale's inflated ERA was simply poor luck. Kershaw, on the other hand, enjoyed the opposite effect.

Kershaw, according to FIP, did a worse job of handling his "non-action" plays, in other words, plays in which no one else needs to get involved. However, his ERA was over one half of a run, 0.59 runs to be exact, lower than Sale's (2.31 to 2.90). Since Kershaw and Sale's defenses were both equally stalwart, all we can discern is that Kershaw simply had a luckier season.

Now, am I saying Kershaw is a worse pitcher than Chris Sale? No. Am I saying that ERA is stupid? Also no. All that I'm saying is that FIP is more concrete as a way to measure what a pitcher does on their own without any influence from other players and that ERA is more susceptible to luck or outliers. This was not an example to place one pitcher above another in terms of overall ability, but rather to show the inefficiencies of ERA as opposed to FIP.

To further demonstrate this, we just need to go back and look at the chart that simulated Kershaw's totals had he pitched 214 innings, as Sale did. FIP takes into account strikeouts, BB/HBP, and home runs. Based on that chart, you'll see that Kershaw, by rate, gave up more home runs with far fewer strikeouts, while allowing slightly less BB than Sale. Naturally, if a pitcher allows more home runs than another, then that aspect of their job is being done less effectively. If a pitcher strikes out far fewer hitters, the same could be said there. Considering Kershaw did both of those, it stands to reason that his FIP would be higher than Sale's.

However, statistically, Sale's season was objectively better. Sale pitched more innings, struck out far more per nine IP, allowed fewer hits/9, HR/9 and walked a similar amount of hitters per nine IP. So how then, beyond something else coming into play, would Sale's ERA be higher than Kershaw's? The unreliability and dependence on others necessary for ERA to take shape is the primary culprit in this particular whodunit. Luck contributes, positively or negatively, far more to ERA than FIP.

FIP essentially takes luck out of the equation. If the pitcher does what he can do, then his FIP reflects it. If a pitcher does a poor job of handling his responsibilities, his FIP reflects that as well. There is no room for poor defensive positioning, poor defensive play, or a 65mph duck fart that gets down with runners on second and third. ERA allows these things to influence its final reading and due to that, I find FIP to be a better measurement of pitcher performance. And to be honest, I don't even dislike ERA like some other FIP proponents. I find the ability to limit earned runs to be extremely important for a pitcher, and I think it gives a good insight into how a pitcher handles jams and other situations in a game setting and over the course of a season. However, when we're determining who did *their* job the best, there needs to be a concrete way to weed out external influences (i.e. defense, luck, sequencing of hits, etc.), and FIP is the best way to do that.

There have been notable examples of pitchers' ERA and FIP totals being what seems to be worlds apart in terms of point differential and categorical quality. In a graphic obtained from Beyond the Box Score by SBNation, you can see some extreme cases of large gaps between ERA and FIP. The original chart has 10 examples, but I've decided to condense it to the three most startling examples.

Pitcher	Team	Year	ERA	Rank	FIP	Rank	Difference	Team dWAR
Chris Bosio	MIL	1987	5.24	75	3.38	8	+1.86	-4.3
John Burkett	TEX	1998	5.68	91	3.89	25	+1.78	1.4
R. Nolasco	FLA	2009	5.06	74	3.35	15	+1.71	-5.5

These three examples are all 11 years apart, so as to indicate that this is not a new problem. Some other significant gaps date all the way back to 1964. But as you can see, there are significant gaps that are possible between ERA and FIP. In the prior graphic, you can see that all three examples were basically outside the top 75 among qualifying pitchers (based on IP). All three are essentially in the top five *worst* in ERA for their given season ("essentially" only because Burkett was sixth worst), yet all their FIP in the same seasons were generally near the top. If you take a look at the farthest-right column, you'll have the likely answer as to why.

dWAR[12] stands for "Defensive WAR," and is used to determine how many wins above a league average player a given player contributes with their defensive play alone. The team dWAR of all three of the teams in our example are either bad or actually worse than replacement level. The 1998 Texas Rangers is the only team in our example that has a dWAR above 0.0, but the team total of 1.4 is hardly stellar. Going back to the Chris Sale/Clayton Kershaw example, the Dodgers, who ranked second in baseball in 2017, had a team dWAR of 5.4. The other two teams' dWAR were both more than four wins *worse* than a team full of replacement-level players. It's no wonder there were so many earned runs that snuck through! These pitchers were, in relation to the rest of the league, doing their job well. The issue was that the team behind them performed so poorly, that the numbers were skewed to the point that the pitchers appeared to be among the league's worst. In many of the examples from the original graphic, the pitchers included were actually dead last in the league in ERA. Obviously, in the case of our three examples, based on their FIP this was not the case as they controlled what they could control as well as almost anyone in the league during their respective seasons. These numbers further illustrate the unreliability of ERA in relation to FIP.

In all my years as a player I heard the phrase, "Control what you can control." The amount of times I've used this phrase in my coaching career perhaps exceeds the amount of baseballs I've thrown during BP. However, it's a cliché because it's true and it's stood the test of time.

---

[12] FanGraphs

For a baseball player to be successful, given how variable the game is and how many aspects simply elude their control over the course of a game, they need to be able to focus only on that which they can control. You can't control umpires, you can't control weather and you can't control the shortstop with a hole in his glove behind you or the fact that the guy coach put in left field tripped on a blade of grass and cost the team two runs. So, if a player is able to maintain focus on only making *their* pitch or winning *their* AB, then they will put themselves in a much better position to have success. It's stuck around forever because it truly applies and is an adage with a message worth heeding.

How then, if we've stressed this concept to players since they've first picked up a ball, can we not measure their performance based on their ability to do just that? FIP is the ultimate "control what you can control" metric. It only measures what the pitcher can do by himself, and therefore is the best look at his individual performance, independent of any outside supplement or detriment provided by the team around him. Again, I recognize that baseball is a team game, and I believe playing to your team and its strengths is important. With that being said, though, if you want to measure a player based on what they've done by themselves, your means of doing so cannot also include what other people do which could affect that measurement.

PART 4
The Drawbacks of Sabermetrics

E veryone get ready, I'm about to say the thing that you should not say in today's baseball world. It's the equivalent of *A Christmas Story*'s, "queen-mother of dirty words" as it relates to baseball analytics allegiances. Don't tell my mom, she might wash out my mouth with soap...

I don't completely love sabermetrics.

Whew, there I said it. Not to say I hate sabermetrics and the new analytics movement in baseball, but I'm just not completely sold on a lot of the metrics that have become household names in today's game. Again, I've stated before that I'm reluctant to accept things I can't see and/or calculate myself. As I've also stated before, that doesn't necessarily make it bad, granted it's explained and broken down in a way that allows me to see behind the curtain and understand what actually goes into creating that statistic. Some of them, though, have yet to make it blatantly clear what they're about or exactly how they're measured. Due to that, I personally find them to be metrics I would choose not to employ. I have to stress again that the aim of this book is not to establish myself as a foremost expert on the various means used to measure baseball performance or to "debunk" anything. This is simply an explanation of my opinion on some of the popular metrics of yesteryear and the modern game, and how I feel they do or do not apply.

So with that in mind, let's jump right in and take a look at some of the aspects of the modern analytics movement and see what leaves something to be desired. Can we beat the machines? Let's find out!

75

Chapter 9
Make ~~love~~ <u>wins</u>, not WAR

T^{*raitor!*}

raitor!
I know that I used WAR in the benefits section, however, it is my opinion that in some cases, WAR misses the mark. It is a raw calculation in a game chock full of human elements and moving parts that cannot be quantified by plugging them into a formula and posting them in a graphic on MLB Network. WAR is a good way to look at player production in a vacuum, but I think that if you expand WAR and use it to start looking at things like team performance, it begins to miss a lot of the very important things that go into what creates good baseball.

In my opinion, WAR is generally not a reliable measurement of a team and the quality of that team. In theory, you should be able to add up all the WAR of all the players of a given team during a season and use the cumulative WAR to determine what their record would be. However, this is not the case. Some teams are able to effectively defy the WAR odds and be better (or worse) than "the algorithm" presents them to be. If you look at some of the most surprising winning teams, you can see that WAR is *never* the answer. To demonstrate this point, we'll take a look at the 2014 World Champion San Francisco Giants.

In 2014, the San Francisco Giants became just the sixth team to make the playoffs as a Wild Card and go on to win the World Series that same season. For those that don't know, in Major League Baseball, there are three divisions per league (National League East, Central and West, and the same for the American League). The winners of each division automatically makes the postseason, with two additional teams per league earning a place via the Wild Card berth, as of 2014. Prior to 2014, there was one Wild Card team that made the playoffs, and that team automatically received a berth to the League

Division Series. The Wild Card is determined by best overall record. The two NL and AL Wild Card teams play in a one-game, winner-take-all playoff to advance the League Division Series.

Anyway, the Giants made the playoffs as one of the Wild Cards, as they didn't win the National League West Division that season. They finished the season with an overall record of 88-74 (.543 win %). However, had WAR had a say, they would have been significantly worse, in fact they would have missed the playoffs altogether, eliminating their World Series run from existence in the baseball cosmos.

For reference, a 0.0 WAR team is the equivalent of a team full of replacement level players. Such a team would be expected to finish with a .294 winning percentage (48-114 over 162 games). By adding up the WAR of every player that played for the Giants in 2014, the team had a total team WAR of approximately 33[13].

If you take those 33 wins and add them on to a 48-114 team, you come up with a record of 81-81, exactly .500. Now, if you'll recall, the 2014 Giants actually finished the season with a record of 88-74, which is seven wins higher than the total their WAR would indicate. Now, you might be thinking to yourself, "Seven wins isn't *that* much." Let's see exactly how significant a seven-win difference truly is.

Thinking back to the first mention of WAR in this book, FanGraphs provides a chart that illustrates WAR totals and their equivalent in terms of their expected role on a Major League roster. That chart read as follows:

Designation	WAR
Scrub	0-1
Role Player	1-2
Solid Starter	2-3
Good Player	3-4
All-Star	4-5
Superstar	5-6
MVP	6+

---

[13] WAR data via Baseball Reference

According to this graphic, seven wins for one player is a season that is a potential MVP-type year. Adding or losing that would be significant to your team. For some reference, here is a list of some seven-win players from the 2014 season:

Player	Notable Stats
Josh Donaldson	29 HR, 98 RBI, 2nd in Def. WAR
Corey Kluber	2014 Cy Young winner
Adrian Beltre	.324 Batting Average
Michael Brantley	.327, 20 HR, 97 RBI

Seven wins would essentially be the equivalent of adding a .300+ hitter, a 30 HR/100 RBI bat, or a player that did both simultaneously. It would also be as if you added a Cy Young-caliber pitcher to your roster. The only difference is in this example, adding the seven-win player wouldn't require a corresponding move, i.e. optioning a player to Triple-A. It would be like adding Corey Kluber in the midst of a Cy Young season to your existing rotation and pitching with a six-man rotation instead of the standard five all season. That, or you're in essence adding Josh Donaldson the year before he won American League MVP honors, or Michael Brantley the season he finished third in MVP voting and adding one of them to your lineup and hitting with 10 players all year. Any GM that wouldn't take that is not one I want making moves for my franchise.

So, the difference between 81-81 and 88-74 is significant in that it's basically the same as adding a star player and playing the whole season one man up on the opposition. Sounds like fun, but I think the mood would change drastically if the tables were turned and a team ends up playing a man *down*, and that man happens to be a Josh Donaldson, Michael Brantley or Corey Kluber. But that's not all.

If the Giants won seven games less, as we calculated, they would have been 81-81. The actual 2014 National League Wild Card Standings ended up looking like this:

Team	W	L	Win %	GB
Pittsburgh Pirates	88	74	.543	-
San Francisco Giants	88	74	.543	-
Milwaukee Brewers	82	80	.506	6
New York Mets	79	83	.488	9

The Giants were tied with the Pirates, and as of 2014, two teams were able to make the postseason via Wild Card berth, so both teams popped champagne. The Brewers were six games back, meaning they had to win six more games over the course of the season to match the Giants and Pirates. However, if you're adept at math, you know that seven is greater than six. So, what happens if the Giants were seven games worse than they actually finished during the 2014 season? The standings change, and they look like this:

Team	W	L	Win %	GB
Pittsburgh Pirates	88	74	.543	-
Milwaukee Brewers	82	80	.506	-
San Francisco Giants	81	81	.500	1
New York Mets	79	83	.488	3

The Giants would not have made the playoffs and someone else would have won the World Series. Pitcher Madison Bumgarner wouldn't have had the opportunity to pitch lights out and earn World Series MVP honors, with his five-inning relief appearance to close out Game Seven forever launching him into folk hero status. On top of all this, the franchise would not have capped off their three titles in five years run that established them as the most successful and decorated franchise of the 2010s. No other franchise has won multiple World Series titles in this decade, let alone three. The difference seven wins can make, huh?

Another example of WAR failing to quantify a team's ability would be an example thus far in the 2018 season. The Washington Nationals are, on paper, one of the best rosters in Major League Baseball.

On paper.

Unfortunately for them, the game is not played on paper. The game is played on dirt and grass, and on dirt and grass they have under-achieved. As of this writing, the Nationals are 71-72 (.497 win %). However, their team WAR would assert they are better on paper than they actually are.

The Nationals' combined WAR is approximately 34. Once again, a 0.0 WAR team would be 48-114 over 162 games. However, since the Nationals have only played 143 games so far in the 2018 season, a .294 winning percentage over 143 games is a record of 42-101. 34 wins above that record would be 76-67, five games better than the Nationals *actual* record. We know the significance of seven wins from the '14 Giants, but five wins isn't as big a deal as seven wins, right? According to our chart from FanGraphs, a five-win player is in the range from all-star to superstar player, so judge for yourself. Either way, let's take a more specific look at the magnitude of a five-win difference.

There are a lot of household names who are currently five win play-ers so far during the 2018 season. To name a few: Colorado Rockies' SS Trevor Story, who will surely have a 30 HR/100 RBI season, but who also has a legitimate chance at joining the 30/30 club, or 30 HR and 30 SB in the same season, making him only the 40th player to ac-complish the feat.

Other five-win players are former Cy Young winners Justin Verlander of the Houston Astros and Corey Kluber of the Cleveland Indians. Both pitchers are perennial Cy Young candidates and have been aces on their respective teams for the better part of this decade.

2017 AL MVP Runner-up Aaron Judge of the New York Yankees is also having a five-win season, as are Chicago Cubs INF Javy Báez, St. Louis Cardinals 1B Matt Carpenter and Milwaukee Brewers OF Christian Yelich, all three of whom are serious candidates for the National League MVP.

So, losing five wins would be the equivalent of simply dropping one of these players from your roster and replacing them with a 0.0 win player. Not what you want for a team to be successful. According to what would be expected from WAR, the Nationals should be successful as if they, in fact, had such an additional player on their roster, so why does their record indicate they're actually playing without him?

Why, even when they have been good, and they have been good, winning four of the last seven National League East Division titles, haven't they been able to win a single post-season series this decade? Why have they had four different managers since 2011, while five different franchises have had just one in that same span? The answer is something that WAR doesn't measure and can't take into account: the fact that this game is played by human beings.

Human beings are fickle. They are susceptible to fatigue, even injury as well as emotions and no two players are the same. WAR has shown to undervalue teams that end up winning and overvalue teams that underachieve. Not to mention, this "replacement player" we keep hearing about is fictitious, he doesn't exist! They phrase it as, "...a player just called up from Triple-A," but we all know that not all players freshly called up from Triple-A are built the same. For example, the Los Angeles Dodgers' Yasiel Puig and Cincinnati Reds' Jay Bruce exploded out of the gate when first called up.

Puig started his career with 27 hits in his first 15 games, which is tied for second highest total all-time through a player's first 15 games, and 34 hits in his first 20 games, which *is* the highest total all-time through a player's first 20 games. He finished the season hitting .319 with 19 HR and 42 RBI in 109 games.

Jay Bruce started similarly hot. In his first week, he hit .577 with three HR, three 2B, seven RBI and 12 runs scored in seven games. He finished the season with 21 HR and 52 RBI in 108 games. In addition, the Reds were 23-28 (.451) before Bruce was called up, but were 5-2 (.714) in his first week in the big leagues. He was a "replacement" player, but he was the one providing wins above someone else.

On the other hand, some players fresh up from Triple-A struggle, take Hall of Famer and some people's GOAT (Greatest of All-Time), Willie Mays. Mays was called up to the New York Giants in 1951 and started his career 0-12. However, in his 13th AB, he did hit a HR off fellow Hall of Famer Warren Spahn. Spahn later joked,

"I'll never forgive myself. We might have gotten rid of Willie forever if I'd only struck him out."

He didn't, and 3,283 hits, 660 HR and 20 all-star game appearances later, Mays is one of the greatest players to ever play the game.

Despite the fact that Willie Mays became one of the best to ever grace a baseball field, the fact is he started his career 0-12, which for many players has spelled the end of their only audition in the big leagues, while Puig and Bruce set the world on fire and have remained productive – though not dominant – major league players is indicative that the term "replacement player" is subjective. It just goes to show you that no two "replacement" players just called up from Triple-A are the same, and so it's difficult at times to accept the validity of the stat when projecting a player or a team's success based on WAR.

When it's all said and done, WAR definitely has its benefits. It is accurate when it comes to who ends up with post-season awards and is one of the only statistics that includes every facet of a player's game. However, in terms of totaling for a team's WAR to determine how much better a team's roster is than a roster of replacement players, it is inaccurate. This is, in my opinion, mainly because WAR is built in a computer. It's not in the clubhouse with the players and it weighs 19-year old uber-prospects and 34-year old, 12-year minor leaguers getting their first taste of the show the same way as they are both being called up for the first time; they are "replacement players." This is simply not accurate and I believe it skews WAR. On a small scale like a single season rating, maybe not so much. However, when taking a team's roster over a whole season, which sometimes exceeds 40 players, it creates gaps. Air-tight, data-driven metrics that are sworn by as more effective, accurate and overall better than traditional measures simply cannot have holes in their measurements the size of MVPs and Cy Young winners.

Chapter 10
"Save" me the trouble:
What exactly is DRS?

H ere comes the fun part for me. Anyone who knows me knows that the defensive side of baseball makes me salivate. It was my strong suit as a player and it is something I value highly as a coach. Defense, in my opinion, has become somewhat of a lost art in baseball today, mainly because great defense isn't sexy. Making great *plays* could grace a magazine cover, however, as with anything else in baseball, greatness lies merely in consistency.

Being a good defensive player over the course of a Major League season requires you to make hundreds upon hundreds of routine plays. You know the type: five-hop ground balls that seemingly roll right into your glove or a can of corn fly ball that requires you to move exactly zero inches. These are the types of plays that need to be made to be a great defender, because the spectacular plays that end up on the postgame highlight reel come around a few times every season at most. It is my assertion that because of that, measuring defense has grown at a rate far slower than that of offense. Why? Because offense is fun! Home runs with bat flips make us want to talk and pitchers throwing 102mph fastballs with arm-side run make us want to find out just how good that guy is. Watching a guy field 500 routine ground balls a season leaves us with, "Well, he only booted 10 of them, so, .980. I guess he's good." With that has been born some metrics that I feel overly-complicate the art of defense, not the least of which is Defensive Runs Saved, or DRS.

DRS is used to calculate exactly how many runs above average any player is for their position. As a refresher, here is the chart displaying various categories of DRS:

Defensive Rating	DRS
Gold Glove Caliber	15+
Great	10
Above Average	5
Average	0
Below Average	-5
Poor	-10
Awful	-15

For starters, my first issue is that the metric is improperly named. Defensive Runs Saved doesn't actually measure the amount of runs a defender saves over the course of a season, rather it measures how many runs *above average* a player is. So, why not Defensive Runs Above Average? dRAA? It's Defensive WAR except translated into runs. Defensive Runs Saved, by name, would be something much different. But that's not really a big deal, however misleading.

When it's all said and done, DRS seems to be throwing too many numbers into the pot when quantifying defense. According to FanGraphs, among other things, DRS measures:

Stolen Base Runs Saved (rSB)
Bunt Runs Saved (rBU)
Double Play Runs Saved (rGDP)
Outfield Arms Runs Saved (rARM)
HR Saving Runs Saved (rHR)
Plus Minus Runs Saved (rPM)

Each of these are used to measure a different facet of a player's defensive game. I feel as though we're slightly overcooking things here. This kind of relates to the whole WAR argument where numbers are being generated from intangible means. Defense is difficult to measure accurately because such a large portion of it comes down to things that are intangible, or at least subject to judgment, such as range.

Range is just how much ground you can cover to make plays. Some guys have poor range, so any ball hit more than three steps to either side is a hit, and some guys have phenomenal range, so any ball hit in the same hemisphere as them results in an out. These are tough to quantify in any objective sense because there's no real way to determine what a player's true range is. Some days they get to a ball that the next day they may not be able to make a play on. Batter's speed plays into this conundrum as well.

In my opinion, all the runs saved via different avenues of defensive play are unnecessary. It's really as simple as:

How many balls are hit to you?
How many more/less batted balls do you field than average?
Of those, how frequently do you convert them into outs?

If you can also account for the rate at which a player's pitching staff induces ground balls or fly balls, then you really have everything you need to know in terms of what can be quantified without someone in a sky box saying, "He should've had that!"

I don't think fielding runs, throwing runs, runs saved and the dozen other hypothetical or league/park/era-adjusted calculations that go into DRS really need to factor in that much. In my opinion, a simple cocktail of Fielding Percentage and Range Factor tells me what I need to know about a defender.

Fielding Percentage is simply the total plays you make divided by the total chances. In other words, the formula is:

$$Fielding\ Percentage = (PO+A)/(PO+A+E)$$

PO is putouts, or how many times a ball you catch or tag that you apply results in an out. A is assists, or how many balls you throw to someone else that result in an out once they catch the throw (and apply a tag, if necessary) and E is errors, or plays the official scorer thought you should have made, but didn't. In other words, a ground ball to shortstop converted into an out is an assist for the shortstop because he threw the ball and a putout for the first baseman because the out occurred once he caught the ball.

Fielding Percentage has been a statistic used for measuring defense for as long as defense has existed in baseball. It's the Batting Average of defense, so naturally, it has come under intense scrutiny. However, while I understand, I also don't know what everyone's huge problem is. I don't know when knowing how frequently a player gets hits became unimportant, and I don't know when knowing how frequently a defender makes plays became something not worth knowing. I know that there is more that goes into playing defense than that, however, to be honest, it's really not that much more. My second piece to the puzzle would be adding Range Factor to the equation.

Range Factor,[14] or RF, has two measures: per game played and per nine innings. All Range Factor measures is how many A and PO a given player makes per game or per nine innings played. So, if a player has a .990 fielding percentage (99% of balls are converted to outs), but their Range Factor indicates that, at their position, they don't make that many plays, then it can be assumed that they primarily make their living on making the routine plays and probably don't have great range. On the other hand, if a player has a slightly worse Fielding Percentage, but has a Range Factor that is much higher than average, you could infer that they make a lot of plays that other players don't, and those errors are the result of them making a play on balls that other defenders don't even get to, absolving them of some blame for the increase in errors.

The combination of those two check our boxes of how many balls a player gets to and the percentage of those balls which they are able to convert into outs. By comparing numbers, you can decide whether a player's numbers are above or below average. For some reference, here are average Fielding Percentages and Range Factors by position from 2017:

---

[14] Range Factor data by Baseball Reference

Fielding % by Position		Range Factor/9 by Position	
Position	**Avg. Fielding %**	**Position**	**Avg. Range Factor/9**
C	.993	C	8.18
1B	.994	1B	8.27
2B	.983	2B	4.22
3B	.966	3B	2.41
SS	.975	SS	3.96
OF	.986	OF	1.99

Obviously, some positions get more action than others, and some positions see a greater degree of difficulty in their action than others, which accounts for the differences in Fielding Percentage and Range Factor. For example, a huge majority of plays that go on the record for a 1B are putouts. This is because they are credited with a putout every time an infielder fields a ground ball and throws to first and gets the out. Due to this fact, if they are simply able to catch the throws from the other in-fielders and field most ground balls cleanly, their Fielding Percentage will generally be on the higher side compared to players in more high-traffic positions. Shortstops, for example, have a lot of responsibility around the field beyond what happens in their immediate area. Their job description includes, but is not limited to, fielding ground balls, patrolling the infield and shallow outfield on fly balls, setting up and executing cuts and relays, taking throw downs from the catcher on SB attempts, starting and turning double plays, etc., so they will make a lot of errors because they have a lot of high-traffic type of responsibility. This isn't to say that shortstop is a more difficult position than first base, as they both require different skills sets, but the job description of a shortstop is far more conducive to committing errors than a first baseman. Anyway, back to DRS.

One of my issues with DRS is that it doesn't line up with what I would consider common baseball sense or knowledge. If a player makes a lot of plays relative to his peers and does so at a high rate, then naturally he's a good defender and saves runs because he's doing his job (convert-ing balls in play into outs) more frequently and more consistently than his counterparts. However, DRS doesn't necessarily follow this model. Case and point: San Diego Padres' SS Freddy Galvis.

Freddy Galvis is, in my humble opinion, among the best defensive SS in Major League Baseball today. I essentially grew up in the shadow of the Walt Whitman Bridge in South Jersey, so I was born and raised a Phillies fan. I skipped school and went to the World Series parade in 2008 and everything. October 29, 2008 was a good day in 16-year old Dean's world. Reminiscing aside, due to my Phillies fandom as a youth, I watched Freddy Galvis emerge as a Major Leaguer and watched almost every game he played during his first few years in the show. Before I even paid much attention to defensive statistics and metrics, I knew he was a good defender because my eyes told me that he was. He had good range, a good arm to go along with soft hands and the ability to be athletic and improvise and he carried those tools to San Diego when he was traded before the 2018 season. However, in doing some research for this section, I noticed he was actually in the *negatives* in DRS during some of his seasons. According to the chart at the beginning of this chapter, his DRS would leave him somewhere between "below average" and "poor." How could this be? I have no idea of what the reasoning is behind Galvis ever being considered a poor defender, as DRS has. I'd like to plead my case as to why I disagree wholeheartedly.

Freddy Galvis has been an every-day Major League Baseball player since 2015. Since that time, his production defensively has been as follows:

Year	*G at SS*	*Assists*	*Field%* [15]	*RF/9* [16]	*DRS*	*Qual. SS*
2015	146 (11)	398 (12)	.973 (17)	4.14 (15)	-6 (18)	23
2016	156 (5)	407 (8)	.987 (3)	3.96 (14)	5 (10)	24
2017	155 (5)	404 (6)	.989 (1)	4.06 (8)	-5 (17)	20
2018*	147 (1)*	373 (4)	.987 (2)	3.97 (7)	7 (8)	22

*2018 season not yet completed, MLB Rank in parentheses

[15] G, A, F%, DRS & Qualifying SS via FanGraphs
[16] RF/9 via ESPN

As you can see, Galvis, with the exception of 2015 which was his first full season in the Major Leagues, has consistently found himself in the top five in Fielding Percentage and has entered the top 10 in Range Factor. Somehow, though, his DRS was 18th out of 23 qualifying SS in 2015, 10th out of 24 in 2016, and 17th out of 20 in 2017. In 2018, his DRS rank is more in line with the rest of his statistics, so I can't really gripe about that, but three out of four ain't bad, or in this case, ain't good. Just for your information, "qualifying" SS are determined by how much playing time a player receives in relation to the number of games his team plays. Some teams have platoon systems in place, so two or three guys will split time at a position and none of them will play enough to qualify for full-season statistical leaderboards.

In 2015, Galvis was middle of the pack in both Fielding Percentage and Range Factor, but was 18th out of 23 (22nd percentile) in DRS. In 2017, he was first in Fielding Percentage and eighth in Range Factor, yet was five runs below average and was 17th out of 20 qualifying SS (15th percentile)? His worst single-season DRS was -6 in 2015, which ends up, again, between "below average" and "poor," which is completely unbelievable to me. This aggression against Freddy Galvis will not stand!

Now, you may be saying to yourself, "His Range Factor has never been that good, so that's probably why his DRS is so low," and you'd be correct. Partly. Galvis' Range Factor is consistently very average. However, if you take a look at the pitching staffs that Galvis has played behind, you'd see he's actually out-fielding the ground ball rates of his pitchers.

In 2015-2017, the Philadelphia Phillies' pitchers behind which Freddy Galvis played were among the worst in baseball at getting ground balls.

Year	Total Ground Balls	Rank	GB%	Rank
2015	2,131	4	46.06%	21
2016	1,871	25	43.05%	27
2017	1,911	19	44.08%	23

With the exception of 2015, in which the Ground Ball Percentage was still bottom third of the league, the pitchers that Galvis has played behind in this three full (and completed, to date) seasons did a poor job overall of getting ground balls. Galvis essentially did an average job of making plays on ground balls despite the fact that his teams were below average at creating ground balls in the first place. He had to make the most of every opportunity to make a play, because they came about at one of the lowest rates in the league on a yearly basis. This information takes any conversation of Galvis being a "volume fielder" out of the question.

The term "volume-anything" is more prevalent in other sports. In basketball, a volume scorer is someone who scores a lot of points, but it's because they take a *ton* of shots. People accuse some elite scorers such as Russell Westbrook and Carmelo Anthony of being volume scorers because they score a lot of points, but also take a lot of shots, and sometimes their low shooting percentages actually act as a detriment to their team. On the other hand, a player like a LeBron James scores almost as many points as the aforementioned players, but does so at a much more consistent clip. Fielding can sometimes be the same way. Infielders can have an astronomical Range Factor because they're the beneficiaries of a massive amount of ground balls, but they are still inconsistent at making plays, resulting in a less than stellar Fielding Percentage. Fielding Percentage balances out Range Factor in this instance, as Range Factor can balance out Fielding Percentage when a player is cherry picking and making far less plays than their counterparts, but consistently makes those plays, many of which do not really test their ability. The only way Galvis could be considered less than average, or even less than elite for that matter, would have been that he was a volume fielder. He clearly is not.

Despite playing behind less than average ground ball-inducing pitching staffs almost all of his career, he is still consistently among the league's best in total Assists, Fielding Percentage and ends up playing above his ground ball rate to achieve average or slightly above-average Range Factor. So, how on earth has he managed to crack the league's top 10 in DRS only once?

Freddy Galvis creates for himself a ton of chances to make plays despite minimal opportunities over his career, converts an exceptionally high number of those opportunities into outs and does so with remarkable consistency. What else does a player need to do to be above average? Wear a weighted vest? Play shortstop left-handed? Defense truly isn't that complicated. Not nearly as complicated as hitting. You know the situation before the ball is pitched, if the ball is hit to you, you catch it and if there's a throw to make you make the throw. The degree of difficulty changes from play to play, but overall that's about it. It's far more physically difficult than mentally. Besides positioning and knowing hitter tendencies, there isn't as much planning as there is execution that goes into playing defense compared to offense. There's no multi-pitch arsenals with varying speeds to worry about, or pitchers varying times to the plate, etc. So why is DRS so much more complicated than virtually every other metric out there? As I've outlined, it doesn't take more than a few parameters to determine if a defender is good, bad or average.

DRS, besides being inappropriately named, also complicates the measurement of defense to the point of confusion. If a player makes a lot of plays, is consistent at making plays and doesn't utilize the benefit of an enormously above average quantity of ground balls compared to his peers to do so, how can you say he's not good, let alone poor? How can a player like Freddy Galvis, who is consistently among the best in many categories, and is consistently above average in Range Factor despite below average ground ball rates, be rated as below average, not to mention the bottom five of all qualified players at his position? It simply doesn't make sense. Defense is not that complicated. Save me the headache, and let's find a less jumbled alternative to Defensive Runs Saved.

Chapter 11
Not All Parks Are the Same,
so Why Level the Playing Field?

In recent years, a large contributor to many metrics that have been released for public consumption has been "park effects." Park effects is essentially sabermetricians' way of adjusting statistics to prevent players who play in favorable conditions from gaining an unfair advantage over players who hit in a huge park or pitch in a launching pad. However, I don't necessarily think it's effective to adjust a player's numbers because of their home ballpark. Mainly because those players do have an advantage, and that isn't a crime punishable by diminishing their production.

No one ever stopped the game and moved the plate back to 65 feet and asked Randy Johnson to chill out because no one felt comfortable hitting against a 6'10" left-hander throwing 101mph bullets. No one removed an inch or two from the outside corner of home plate because they were helpless against Greg Maddux's backdoor two-seamer, and nobody *ever* told the Murderers' Row Yankees teams of the 1920s that they couldn't let Babe Ruth and Lou Gehrig play on the same field because they were simply too talented to compete against. Gaining an advantage is the whole purpose of sports. I'm all for a level playing field, but especially in outdoor sports, like baseball, players have to play to their surroundings. Different approaches work better with different environments, and park effects essentially eliminate that.

If every player was trying to do the same thing, regardless of where they played, maybe park effects would be appropriate. But you have to play differently in all facets of the game in San Diego than you do in Denver, and because of that, park effects is really comparing apples and oranges when adjusting production. Saying that a guy who is purposely trying to lift the ball doesn't deserve as many HR, while a guy who purposely tries to keep the ball out of the air deserves *more* HR even though that's not what he's going for doesn't really make that much sense to me. That's like saying a team who has a rowdy home crowd that makes it tough on opposing teams deserves 2.563% less wins over the course of a season because the numbers shake out that they earned however-many more wins as a result of their home field advantage. Nonsense!

Granted, some parks are tougher to hit in than others, but some places are tougher to pitch in than others as well, so at the very least you'll have a pitching advantage to balance out your offensive woes. No ballpark is both a hitters' park *and* a pitchers' park, unless your team is bad. However, generally speaking, Major League players know their individual games and know their home park and purposely develop a game plan to have success in that ballpark, and I don't think players who have success based on that should have their numbers dinged as a result.

Coors Field, home of the Colorado Rockies in Denver, Colorado, is one of the most notorious hitter-friendly ballparks in Major League Baseball. With the stadium sitting one mile above sea level, its altitude comes with thin air and allows hitters to add a few extra feet to the back end of their batted balls. Because of this, it has been very difficult for Rockies' players to be considered in the MVP voting, because voters assert that their home ballpark aids their offensive production. While there may be certain innate benefits that come with playing in certain ballparks, I don't think it's the player's fault that they're simply playing to the advantages their ballpark provides. That would be like a hitter knowing a fastball was coming, but not hitting it into the upper deck because it wouldn't have been *fair*. If you have the answers to the test, use them, or they'll pay someone else all those millions of dollars. And in some cases, the adjustments of park effects may cost you a few million. At the end of the day, balls that leave the yard left the yard in real life. It really, actually happened. It's observable in nature and provable through the scientific process, and that's about as real as it gets.

Altering those numbers because of the stadium out of which the ball traveled is essentially attempting to alter reality, which is the last thing any type of measurement that claims to be a more accurate means of measuring and deriving value from any set of data would want.

Math is based in reality, therefore sabermetrics are based in reality, and so changing reality is changing the basis by which these metrics are even generated in the first place. A home run in Colorado is not worth 1.195 HR somewhere else just because it's in Colorado. It's worth one home run because, well, it's one home run. Adding weighted values to outcomes (à la wOBA) is one thing, but actually altering the literal value of the outcomes based on location, topography, etc. is not something I agree with.

To illustrate some of the shortcomings of park effects, let's use players from two polar opposite ballparks. We'll look at Nolan Arenado, third baseman of the Colorado Rockies, who calls the hitter-friendly Coors Field home, and Eric Hosmer, first baseman for the San Diego Padres, who, as of 2018, plays his home games at the pitcher-friendly Petco Park.

Arenado's career splits look like this:

Nolan Arenado Career Splits							
	G	*Avg.*	*OBP*	*SLG*	*H*	*2B*	*HR*
Home	431	.319	.374	.606	525	121	105
Away	428	.265	.320	.472	432	96	77
+ / -	**+3**	**+54**	**+54**	**+134**	**+93**	**+25**	**+28**

It is clear that Arenado enjoys more success in the comfort of his home stadium than he does on the road. Much more success, as a matter of fact. However, is that objectively and definitively because he plays at Coors Field? Many players hit better at home than on the road, for a myriad of reasons. Sleeping in your own bed instead of a hotel, getting the opportunity to go through your standard game-day routine in a familiar city, and no jet-lag from a red eye the night before are just a few aspects that lend themselves to more success at home than on the road. Just because Arenado's home happens to be at one of the most hitter-friendly parks in baseball doesn't necessarily mean his production value is any less than his statistics would indicate (his production is tremendous, and we'll see more of it in just a moment), and by no means should that be a valid reason for him to have as little success in MVP voting as he has had.

Arenado has played his whole career in Colorado, and since 2015, has done as much damage as any player in baseball. In the three full seasons since 2015, he has led the league in HR and RBI twice and is a .297 hitter during that span. His average stat line for that three year span is: .297/.353/.577, 86 XBH (extra-base hits), 40 HR, 131 RBI. In those three seasons, with those numbers, his *best* finish in the MVP voting has been fourth. He's never even been a finalist. For reference, here is Arenado's average season between 2015 and 2017 with the National League MVP winners from each of those season:

Season	Player	Team	AVG	OBP	SLG	HR	RBI
'15-'17	Nolan Arenado	COL	.297	.353	.577	40	131
2015	Bryce Harper	WAS	.330	.460	.649	42	99
2016	Kris Bryant	CHC	.292	.385	.554	39	102
2017	Giancarlo Stanton	MIA	.281	.376	.631	59	132

One would think that one's average season being comparable to basically all three MVP seasons in one way or another during the same span would warrant more than two total first-place votes over three seasons, but, I guess that's why I'm not voting. Arenado plays in Colorado, but year in and year out he puts up great numbers, despite faring much better at home than on the road. But I don't think we should be docking him value just because of where he plays. Plenty of players find comfort at home, even when home is a pitchers' park.

To that point, I'd like to look at Eric Hosmer next. As we stated, he plays in San Diego, in a known pitchers' park in Petco Park. However, he too hits better at home than on the road.

Eric Hosmer 2018 Splits							
	G	Avg.	OBP	SLG	H	2B	HR
Home	70	.280	.347	.439	76	19	8
Away	72	.224	.286	.359	65	11	8
+ / -	-2	+56	+61	+80	+11	+8	-

Thus far in 2018, Hosmer, despite playing at a traditionally pitcher-friendly park, actually has *less* success away from home. He actually has fairly solid numbers at home. However, despite playing in the National League West, he has a tougher time producing away from Petco Park. The significance of playing in the NL West is that 36 of his 81 road games are in Colorado and Arizona (teams play division opponents 18 times every season), which are both traditionally hitters' parks (Arizona had the second and third highest Park Factor for runs scored in '16 and '17, respectively, Colorado was first both seasons). Before we continue on, I'd like to address a question some of you may be asking: What are Park Factors?

Park Factors are essentially a way to quantify which parks are more or less conducive to scoring runs, hitting home runs, etc. They have Park Factors for overall runs scored, hits, XBH, and others. This is an effort to "level the playing field" amongst Major League hitters, pitchers, etc. I'm personally not completely sold on the necessity of Park Factors, but we'll talk about that in just a moment. If I may, I'd like to finish my point on the Eric Hosmer/Nolan Arenado comparison.

As evidenced by the two players' splits, it's evident that playing in a pitcher or hitters' park is not necessarily directly related to a player's performance for the season. Nolan Arenado, naturally, hits better at home than on the road, but the difference between his home/road splits are actually less drastic than that of Hosmer, despite Hosmer playing at, traditionally, one of the worst parks to hit in.

Again, don't get me wrong, I'm not saying that there are not benefits to hitting in certain parks more than others. I'm also not saying I wouldn't rather be a position player in Colorado than San Diego, because neither of those statements would be true. What I am saying, though, is that just because a player plays in Colorado doesn't make his contributions any less significant, or more importantly, *real*, than someone who plays in San Diego. If Eric Hosmer struggles more on the road compared to at home than Nolan Arenado does, then I don't really feel as though taking value away from Arenado is appropriate. He's not gaining any more progression from his mean level of production than Hosmer is. Could it be possible that he's just a better hitter? And could it be possible that Park Factors aren't always dependent on some invisible, intangible home run wizard in the sky magically carrying balls out in favor of players in certain cities? I think so. I believe that while altitude, topography, stadium design, etc. do have something to do with ball flight and, in turn, power production, I also believe that for a park to be conducive to scoring runs, the team that plays in it probably needs to be able to score runs in the first place.

Show your work.

Don't mind if I do!

In 2001, there were (at least) two stadiums that were toward the bottom of the league when it came to their Park Factor for runs scored that were toward the top in 2017. Those were Wrigley Field, home of the Chicago Cubs and Comerica Park, home of the Detroit Tigers. Let's start with the Tigers.

In 2001, Detroit's Comerica Park was 21st in Major League Baseball in Park Factor for runs scored, with a Park Factor of .978, which means that every one run scored in Comerica Park equates to .978 runs scored at a "league average" ballpark during the '01 season, because it was easier to score runs at an average ballpark than at Comerica. However, in 2017, that same stadium was fourth in all of baseball, with a 1.169 Park Factor for runs scored. How is this possible? Did they build a giant fan that sits behind home plate that kicks on in the bottom half of every inning in an effort to propel balls batted by the Tigers' hitters further? Or was the team that played their games in the stadium simply better at scoring runs? I assert the latter to be true. If you look at some of the break down, the 2017 Tigers had a better team OPS (At the risk of sounding like a hypocrite, team OPS has been shown to be far more accurate in terms of matching true production than individual player OPS), scored more runs and hit more HR than the 2001 Tigers, to name a few stats. So, did something about the park change? Or did the team that calls it home simply improve its offensive output? For more evidence we turn to everyone's favorite lovable loser-turned-National League juggernaut, the Chicago Cubs.

In 2001, and keep in mind Sammy Sosa hit 64 HR in 2001, the friendly confines of Wrigley Field were not so friendly, finishing 24th in Major League Baseball with a .930 Park Factor for runs scored. In 2017, those same friendly confines finally lived up to the name, ending up fifth in the game with a 1.131 Park Factor. Again, the 2017 Cubs had a higher team OPS, scored far more runs and hit more HR than the 2001 Cubs. For your viewing convenience, here is a comparison between both the Tigers and Cubs 2001 and 2017 teams[17]:

Chicago Cubs – Wrigley Field					*Detroit Tigers – Comerica Park*				
Year	*Park Factor* [18]	*OPS*	*R*	*HR*	*Year*	*Park Factor*	*OPS*	*R*	*HR*
2017	1.131	.775	822	223	2017	1.169	.748	735	187
2001	.930	.766	777	194	2001	.978	.730	724	139

So, if the team scores more runs than average, the park they play in will also yield more runs than average. I don't necessarily believe that it is the fault of the player if, firstly, they hit in a hitters' park, or secondly, they are on a team that scores a lot of runs, skewing the Park Factor and in turn effectively diminishing their production in the eyes of metrics such as wRC+. Not to mention that Park Factors struggle to quantify the different effects that exist within a single park.

In Yankee Stadium, a left-handed hitter will undoubtedly have a more skewed production of power than a right-handed hitter. Yankee Stadium is 314 feet down the right field line, 362 feet in the right-center

---

[17]Team statistics via Baseball Reference
[18]Park Factor via ESPN

gap, while left field is 346 feet just a few feet to the right of the left field foul pole and 399 feet in the left-center field gap. For context:

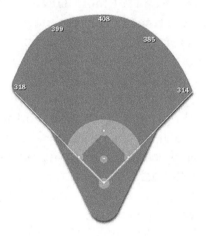

However, there is only one Park Factor for Yankee Stadium. If a right-handed hitter hits a lot of home runs in Yankee Stadium, which is widely regarded as a hitters' park, will he be docked production, even though his pull-side of the field is actually more difficult to hit a home run against than average? The same goes for Boston's iconic cathedral, Fenway Park.

Fenway is interesting because there are many wrinkles to that stadium and its effect on hitters. Down the right field line, the unusually shallow right field corner, punctuated by the even more awkwardly placed Pesky's Pole is a remarkably short 302 feet away from home plate, allowing left-handed hitters to hit for more power than could generally be expected in a park with more general dimensions (average parks are usually approximately 330-335 feet down the lines, 380-385 in the gaps and 400-405 to dead center). However, the Green Monster poses some interesting issues in quantifying park effects.

The Green Monster is a nickname for Fenway Park's famous left field wall. It's shallow in regard to its distance from home plate, sitting 310 feet away. However, it earns its name as "The Monster" by standing 37.2 feet tall. It's the boogieman where line drive home runs go to die. This offers a much different advantage or disadvantage to players, depending on how you look at it.

For a hitter, a tall, shallow fence can change the scope of your season if you play 81 of your games there. The shallow but tall fence has the possibility to turn a 315 foot fly ball which, anywhere else, would likely be a fly out, into a long, high single or double that ricochets off the wall. So, in that sense, it's advantageous to players in that it creates some hits where they may not exist otherwise. However, it can also create an issue for right-handed line drive hitters who are looking to lift some HR. The Monster is only 310 feet from home plate, but its height of 37.2 feet has turned many a home run into a long single over the years. If a player hits a hard line drive, with a launch angle of 17 degrees and an exit velocity of 100mph, a potentially 360+ foot home run ends up being a hard single off the Green Monster, due to the expected max height of that batted ball being only 36 feet. 360 feet down the line is a home run in every ballpark in Major League Baseball (Wrigley Field has the deepest corners with left field being 355 ft. and right field being 353 ft.). So, the Green Monster creates hits, but it also can take home runs away, decreasing overall power production.

How do park effects quantify the different effects that different parts of ballparks have on various types of hitters? Or does it just box in all the numbers and say, "This ballpark is a hitters' park, so anyone who has a huge year here will be dialed back down to where *we* think they would be in an average stadium"? Meanwhile, a right-handed hitter hits 30 line drives off the monster and loses out on several HR, and *still* has his numbers doctored back to a mean level because his field's Park Factor is high because right field would be small, even for a high school field. So, a given park may be conducive to getting hits, but may stifle power production at the same time, and may also be more forgiving depending on the side of the plate a batter hits from. Seems like a lot to quantify into a one-size-fits-all number to grade the park.

All told, I see what park effects are trying to do, and I understand the potential cry out for such a metric, but I don't think it's practical. For one, if one ballpark can go from one of the worst hitters' parks to one of the best in approximately 15 years' time, and vice versa, then

Park Factors aren't reliable overall, as they're subject to such drastic change. Especially if nothing changed except the team playing inside its walls. In addition, there are a lot that goes into why certain hitters hit well at a given ballpark, and often times they have nothing to do with the thin air or ocean breeze blowing in from right field (looking at you, San Francisco). Players like Nolan Arenado in today's game are cast asunder because of the added "benefits" of playing in his home ballpark, while other players enjoy the same level of success hitting in home ballparks that are considered difficult to hit in, but have the value of their numbers boosted. Not to mention, Arenado was drafted by the Rockies and came up through their minor league system, so it wasn't even his choice that Coors is his home field, so it's not like he was knowingly gaining an advantage. He was a high school kid from California who had basically just been written a check for over half a million dollars, so I don't think it was the air density in Denver that had him salivating on draft day.

You can't punish one and reward another based simply off of the reputation of the park in question. So, all in all, park effects are good in sentiment, but possibly overkill and oversight in execution.

Sabermetric Conclusion

Traditional statistics are weather-beaten. They are dirty and worn and frayed around the edges. Sabermetrics are shimmering, shiny chrome that marks the advanced technology of the modern day baseball game. The eye test has widely been replaced by algorithms, and while that can ultimately lead to some problems, overall it is efficient and more thorough than the traditional pencil and paper method.

While, as I said, a younger version of myself took a firm pro-traditional, anti-sabermetric stance, I have lightened up significantly. I've done the research, looked into the numbers and actually given the new metrics a chance and have found a lot of benefit to many of them. However, as with anything, they are not without flaws of their own, despite vehement assertions from their advocates that the output of the various algorithms and formulas are gospel and are to be carved into stone for permanent enshrinement in the mathematics Hall of Fame (is that a thing?). To recap:

WAR accurately aligns with MVP and Cy Young winners, so it absolutely does its job in terms of illustrating overall production in a given season. It's also one of the few metrics that give an all-inclusive look into every facet of a player's game. However, shortcomings do exist, even for the almighty WAR.

I've found that WAR misses out on some of the human effects that contribute to an MLB season, especially in regards to evaluating a team's roster. Frequently, a team's record will not line up with its WAR projection, which as we know is based off of a 0.0 WAR team going 48-114. It sometimes comes close, but can often leave a hole or credit a team contributions worth the value of an MVP or Cy Young winner. As insignificant as that may seem, there's not a GM on planet earth that wouldn't take an extra MVP on their team or mourn the loss of that same MVP to free agency (or the residual effect of inaccurate WAR values). WAR is the face of the sabermetrics community, but overall, despite some holes in its game, I'd value WAR as a beneficial metric, assuming you had the data collection and calculation means to re-create it. An additional, albeit minor flaw is that it's tough for all to utilize because I'm not aware of any high school programs with its own data collection and analytics department, time to call the math club I guess!

wOBA may sound funky, but it's actually fairly basic given the company it keeps. It's essentially a more accurate and a more wide-ranging way of calculating Slugging Percentage. Not all hits are created the same, and wOBA allows for that. Creating different weights for each outcome, it gives a much more accurate look into a player's overall production offensively. Where Slugging Percentage is a good measure of total bases per AB, that metric in itself is limited in range. wOBA takes the same concept and includes BB, HBP and sometimes reaching base via error to calculate how effective a player's offensive game truly is. The benefits to this far outweigh any detriment, as we are now able to encapsulate the most common and important offensive outcomes and measure their contributions to a team's run scoring potential and derive a metric that measures how well a player contributes to that, which we have never had in the past. In addition to that, the formula is remarkably simple to utilize in one's own analytics portfolio, regardless of level. In terms of ease of calculation, if WAR is advanced, theoretical, quantum, mega-calculus, wOBA is long division. I, too, choose long division if given the choice. I'll avoid doing heavy lifting if it isn't necessary. The same can be said for pitchers and their shouldering the burden of sub-par defenses weighing heavily on their ERA.

If you move to the pitching side of things, FIP is the "do-it-yourself" pitcher's best friend. It is a true measurement of a pitcher's individual performance. Being a pitcher is the ultimate solo act in baseball. They are the ones that dictate the game, yet many avenues of measuring their performance involve other players doing their job well. FIP eliminates that. Taking only the outcomes that pitchers have total control over, FIP has allowed us to see exactly how much a pitcher truly handles his burden. A pitcher who has a horrendous defense and one who has a roster full of Gold Glovers can both bring equal value and have that value brought to light through FIP.

Now, as I said, while sabermetrics are shiny and fun, they are not without issues, as the old-school baseball minds will so gleefully point out. While, I don't find joy in asserting my concerns, I do so with confidence as a changed man. Someone who, years ago would have been right on the front lines with the Goose Gossages of the world, picketing with signs that said "NERDS" or "SICK POCKET PROTECTOR," or something equally pompous, I now understand the place of these metrics and can voice my concerns with an unbiased tone.

I've already stated my concerns with WAR, as minimal as they may seem. I will say, though, there is a variability lacking in the sabermetric community for what we call the "human element," (we'll talk about that in just a moment, as well). WAR is no exception. Neither are Defensive Runs Saved or the application of park effects.

Defensive Runs Saved is a metric that overcooks defense. It's really as simple as how many plays you have a chance to make relative to average, how many of those chances you convert to outs relative to average, and adjusting judgment based on the overall quantity of any given batted ball type you see via your pitching staff. Defensive Runs Saved is taking throwing arm runs, stolen base runs and a laundry list of other factors, when guys with bad arms can play great defense and the numbers generally don't line up. With the Freddy Galvis example, a guy who makes more plays than almost everyone, at a higher percentage than almost everyone despite seeing less ground balls than average but still out-producing his pitchers' ground ball rate has had defensive seasons where he is nearly 10 runs *worse* than average? Never. My homer-ism for Freddy Galvis aside, DRS may be a little too smart for its own good. And I know I used DRS in some examples over the course of the book, but that's just due to the fact that it is a commonly accepted metric that people knew how to read.

Moving on to park effects, my main issue with them is that they punish and reward players for things that often aren't their fault or really in their control. Players need to play to their environment, and leveling the playing field would indicate that all players have the same approach and do things the same way, regardless of where they play which is obviously not the case. Baseball is hard enough as it is, no need to dock guys points because of where their home park is.

Overall, I'm much more a fan and proponent of the sabermetric movement than I used to be. I think, objectively, the new analytics sector of baseball does a good job quantifying very small, even seemingly inconsequential aspects of play and framing them in a way that adds value to them. While I do think sometimes they're overcooked or presented either in a way that's tough to get people to dig in on (rename RE24, seriously), or are done in such a smug way it makes people who love the game as it is not want to hear what is being said.

To summate, all this book is, is a conversation. No one is completely right and no one is completely wrong. Traditionalists and sabermetricians can call off the regularly scheduled West Side Story-esque gang fight. It all matters, and both come up short.

Conveniently enough, where one argues the other is lacking, his or her side usually has the means to pick up the slack, to which neither side is likely to ever admit. Either way, it's very useful to have such a vast array of measurements at our disposal, and it's a good problem to have and one unique to baseball. While the conversation isn't over, I've presented my arguments for and against both sides. What I think is appropriate next is for me to attempt to bridge the gap. With all the information that has been presented, how can we know which stats to use, which to ignore and which ones can work in harmony to provide the best and most accurate view of the game?

PART 5
Practical Application

I understand that I've just thrown a lot of information at you. Hopefully it all made sense and hopefully it shed some light on the pros and cons of the various statistics and methods of analyzing player production, but I do still understand that there's a lot of information that I've left for you to process.

I thought I would take this next section and attempt to unpack a lot of the thoughts and opinions I've just presented. I hope I've armed you with enough information and evidence to make your own decisions, but I thought it would be an interesting idea if I broke down a little bit of how I incorporate the new metrics with old statistics and (attempt to) maintain a balance between the two in my own analysis of my players.

Again, and as I've stated before, I don't claim this to be the gospel in terms of how to apply all these numbers, and I'm always open to discussion and different interpretations of things so that I can develop a stronger understanding and means by which to apply these numbers in evaluating players. As anyone who coaches or has attempted to assign value to players based on things that they see as valuable knows, it is no easy undertaking. It's difficult to, firstly, attempt to collect enough information to have a meaningful bank of data by which to analyze players, especially at lower levels. As I said earlier, I don't know any high schools that have an analytics department that collects, mines, organizes and presents all relevant data to the coaching staff for their in-game convenience. So, it's left to the coaches to then find what aspects of play they value, measure it, and find a way to present it in a way that makes sense to the staff, players, parents and sometimes the colleges or professional scouts that have their eye on that player. Oh, and on top of all of that they have to actually coach the team.

If everyone reads this section and determines that I'm 100% full of crap and decides they don't agree with any of my methods of applying all the various statistical measurements that we've discussed, then fine. But I just want to throw some of these things out there, because it would have probably helped me in some way when I was trying to figure out what on earth was going on when I first ventured to decipher all the weighted, plus, expected, run-value-based linear weight models-type numbers that were served to me on a not-so-silver platter a couple of years back.

For some reference, I am the head coach of a high school baseball team in Tulsa, Oklahoma. I was the assistant coach at the same high school for two seasons prior to my being promoted, and I suppose that I developed somewhat of a reputation around the locker room as being a "stat guy." Now, before I dispute that, I have to disclose that during the season, any day which we don't have a game, I pull up to practice with a, usually close to 10-page thick, packet of updated stats. Everything from team defense to stolen base efficiency, various offensive categories, etc. I've spent *a lot* of time developing Excel spreadsheets with formulas built in so I can plug and chug in-season, so much so that I sometimes hear my computer let out a big sigh when I ask it to open Excel, but that's between me and my MacBook.

I don't show up with that much information because I want all of our players to mull over every number in there and give themselves vertigo, but rather because I want a large pool of data to pick from when it comes time to analyze it as a coach. The numbers tell a story in my opinion, and I want to have as close to a complete version of that story as possible when looking at what needs to improve. Doing a lot for my, "I'm not a stat guy," case, I know.

Truly, though, I don't feel that I am. Even as a player, I definitely kept an eye on my stats, but not because I loved math, but rather because I wanted a full-scope view of what was happening during my season. Same as a coach.

For example, if I notice that we're facing a lot of hitters per innings pitched, but are not throwing very many pitches per hitter, then maybe our pitch sequencing is becoming predictable and guys are jumping on us, or our quality of strike isn't good enough and we need to get back to working the corners instead of trying to just blow guys away. It may seem a bit like overkill to know how many pitches we throw per hitter, but it led to a significant adjustment during our 2018 spring season that led to our pitchers performing much better during the back half of the season.

Long story short, I think understanding what your numbers are saying is important. I also think using various statistics to piggy-back off one another can give coaches or even just the mathematically-inclined fan a better look and better understanding of what the numbers are saying, because I think understanding is obviously more important than simply collecting and presenting. Having a purpose behind what metrics or statistics you value and collect is as important as being able to actually collect them.

So, here goes nothing. I'm prefacing this by acknowledging I'm still learning and if anyone reads this and wants to contact me, slide in my DMs, whatever the case may be to offer their two cents on how I could improve or streamline my assessments, by all means, be my guest. However, as it stands now, this is how I use them and I've found that it's allowed for some potentially difficult metrics to become easier to swallow in the midst of all the other responsibilities that come with being a coach.

Chapter 12
Out With the "Old"

Since I spent so much time outlining the negative aspects of many of the metrics that have become commonplace, it's only natural that there are several that I no longer include in the statistics that I keep. Which is certainly saying something, because I keep *a lot* of statistics for my team.

As I said, I became "stat guy" due to my, shall we say, tendency to keep a "thorough" stat portfolio. It wasn't as difficult as you would think, either, just a few small charts that I kept pinned to a bulletin board in the dugout in which I'd write tally marks after each batter, or a card I kept in my pocket while coaching, where I'd mark the result of each AB. It truly didn't feel cumbersome and didn't feel as though I was compromising my ability to actually coach during the game.

Anyway, developing my beliefs and theories on what I value as a coach, there are certain statistics that I have begun to stay away from when I collect and present my statistics to my fellow coaches and my team. I'd like to discuss a few of the main ones, just for a short time.

The first statistic I have omitted from my stat sheets is pitchers' wins and losses. Like that comes as any surprise. I shouldn't say that I don't keep it, per se, because I do keep track of it, simply because it's asked to be included when schools are recruiting or putting feelers out for certain players, but it holds almost no weight when I'm evaluating my pitchers, and never more than, "Oh cool, such-and-such is 7-0."

As I've stated, wins and losses for a pitcher are only as valuable as the degree to which you allow external factors to infiltrate and influence your measurements, so I choose not to include it when presenting it to my guys. If they ask, generally I put on my coach face and say something to the effect of, "The team is [insert W/L record here], and that's what matters," just like the coach you and I both couldn't stand playing for. Though, at the end of the day, that's all that really does matter to me. I need to win baseball games, I wasn't hired to babysit, so while I'm thrilled for Johnny that he's 7-0, and trust me, I'm as thrilled as anyone if not more so, if Johnny's seven wins are the only ones we have as a team, then Johnny's wins are not really doing anything to accurately indicate our team's performance. Sure, I could see that maybe we're hitting a little better behind Johnny than our other pitchers, or that our defense is more stout when he's on the mound. But guess what? I can't tell that from wins alone. All I know from pitching wins is how many wins Johnny has. So if I can find a metric that better indicates Johnny's individual performance while simultaneously getting a picture of what our team is doing differently with Johnny on the mound, why would I not use that in lieu of wins and losses? I don't find it to be effective to keep statistics in an effort to measure a player's performance when it requires many other players also doing their job for that statistic to even exist.

The next statistic I don't really keep other than for disclosure in the recruiting process is RBI. Now, I don't hate RBI *nearly* as much as many of those loyal folks who pledge their allegiance to sabermetrics, but I also don't love it as much as many of the traditionalists who cling to it.

Side note: many people think RE24 (Run-Expectancy Based on the 24 Base-Out States) is better than RBI, and it may be, I'm not sure. However, as an adult of sound body and mind, I am consciously choosing to take the low road, be petty and simply refusing to acknowledge it until they figure that name out. I mean, c'mon. Like, just call it Total Adjusted Run Production, "TARP," or, I don't know, literally anything else. Maybe I'm being a bit hypocritical, but I'm taking a stand on this one!

Sorry, like I said, rabbit holes. All kidding aside, back to RBI!

I chose not to include RBI in the anti-traditionalist section of this book because I do see the value in it. The rub is, I just see too much subjectivity in it to really *love* it like I used to. Much like pitcher wins,

RBI rely on a lot of other people doing things right for a player to have an elite total. For example, Mike Trout, the best player in the game has played six full Major League Baseball seasons (2018 excluded). He has eclipsed 100 RBI *twice*, despite being a .323 hitter with runners in scoring position, which is 16 points higher than his overall career Batting Average of .307. He's hit 30 HR four times and led the league in OBP and SLG multiple times each as well, yet only amassed 100 RBI twice. Most of this has to do with the fact that his team, the Los Angeles Angels, have been less than stellar as a team since his call-up in 2011, going 590-544 (.520), and consistently landing in the bottom 10 in Major League Baseball in team OBP, only cracking the top 10 in the three seasons from 2012-2014, with Mike Trout having been in the Major Leagues since 2011. Obviously, they are generally not setting the table all that much. Perhaps not so coincidentally, Trout had his first, third and fourth highest career RBI totals in 2012 (83), 2013 (97) and 2014 (111).

In addition, Bryce Harper, widely regarded as one of the elite sluggers in the game, has *never* reached the 100 RBI milestone in any completed season (again, 2018 excluded).

So, RBI is generally pretty dependent on others, so I don't find it to be all that useful in determining how my players are performing, or how our team as a whole is swinging the bat.

One instance when RBI might be useful in a team evaluation sense is understanding how our team performs with runners in scoring position. One of our main focuses is being able to focus and cash in runs when we are in a position to do so, but there are more specific means of determining how the team is doing in that situation. When we keep our charts, we designate when that AB takes place with a runner in scoring position, so we get direct feedback of how our players perform (AVG, SLG, etc.) with runners in scoring position. We also are able to track our runs total and runs per game. That's easy though, just know the final score of each game and divide the runs by games played. However, simple or not, all of that is more specific and tells a better story of run production than RBI. Plus, especially in the lower levels of baseball, it's fairly easy to guess where most of your team's RBI will end up coming from.

Your best athletes are generally going to be the best hitters, and your best hitters are going to do the most damage. Sometimes, there are outliers when a surprise player gets a higher total of RBI than what would be anticipated, but we have the means to know if they're actually doing damage with runners on, or they're just grounding out to SS a lot, and there just so happens to be a man on third base a lot of the time. Obviously there's value in creating a run that way, but scoring a run that way is not any kind of indicator that the player in question is producing above their position in the batting order, necessitating them being moved up to the middle of the order. So again, RBI is dependent on a lot of factors, and there are ways to more specifically measure production. With that in mind, let's work our way to the third statistic I've decided not to keep for our team.

Now, this particular statistic is not one that I can really avoid keeping. We've discussed it before, and it exists simply as stacking two statistics on top of each other. That's right, our good old friend, OPS.

As I said, I can't really keep from seeing OPS, as I keep OBP and SLG for our players and team as a whole, however I don't place that much stock into it. As we discussed before, OPS can be mathematically incorrect, with two different denominators simply being added together. However, that's not the main reason I choose not to employ it when discerning value within my team.

Realistically, I don't keep track of OPS because there's no sense in keeping track of a statistic that doesn't actually keep track of anything. I posed the question earlier in the book, "What does OPS actually measure?" And the answer is, really, nothing. Not nothing in that it doesn't say anything at all, because it's the combination of two different measurements, but rather nothing in that there's no true definition for what specific act of baseball OPS measures. It doesn't just measure the frequency with which a player reaches base, because there's the SLG aspect to it, and it doesn't just measure power production, because there's that pesky OBP in there as well. It's sort of a mish-mosh of statistics that have somehow slipped through the cracks of the levee that once held Game-Winning RBI, Holds and countless other metrics on the outside of the baseball statistical stratosphere looking in (too soon?).

As a coach, it's my job to keep things efficient, streamlined. No wasted drills in practice, no wasted time in preparation, no wasted cues or application of scouting, etc. in-game. So why, then, would I take into account a statistic that I have to guess as to what the actual meaning is? Realistically a .800 SLG and a .200 OBP, as well as a .200 SLG and an .800 OBP are both still a 1.000 OPS, even though those hitters are *very* different, and neither hitter is probably a very well-rounded offensive player. And the best part is, you can't even cite the mathematical oddity that those stat lines would be, and they are definitely that, because OPS itself plays by mathematical prison rules as it is! It's a free-for-all! Wee!

Really though, I don't find OPS, while generally effective at relating to overall team production, to be mathematically sound enough, or specific enough to include in a statistic report that I give to my players or coaches.

"Johnny, here's how often you get on base, and how many bases you amass per AB."

"So, Coach, which is it?"

"It's both!"

"I don't understand."

"Neither do I! It's OPS though. It's cool, I promise. Mike Trout's is really good, so…"

I can't, in good conscience, evaluate and grade a player based on a statistic that I don't actually understand, and that no one is logically able to understand because it logically doesn't mean anything specifically or doesn't mathematically make any sense. It's close, and I get what people who use OPS are going for, but it needs a tweak to, in my opinion, be something I can use in good faith to evaluate my players.

Maybe I'll use BAPS or True OPS, but that's a headache for another book. Stay tuned!

The moral of the story here is, when I'm looking to assess the performance and production of my players, if a statistic can't give me an idea of how our team as a whole is performing, then I don't want to waste my time thinking about it. Obviously, knowing my two-hole's

Batting Average isn't necessarily an indication of how the team as whole is performing, but if I see his production slip at the same pace as the guy hitting behind him, then maybe I need to shuffle the lineup a touch and get him some better protection and get my former three-hole hitter a few more fastballs to hit at a lower spot in the lineup. Will it work? Possibly. But if I don't have access to certain information, I can't make an informed decision. I'm as big a fan of the "eye-test" as anyone when it comes to baseball, but I also know the eye-test alone is simply taking a shot based on a feeling or a hunch. When your job is to win, you can't really justify a move by saying, "Meh, I had a feeling." At least I don't think you can.

Coaching is hard as it is, it's a very time-consuming, thought-provoking, brain-rattling heart wrencher of a profession, and it's usually a thankless one at that. Too much to do, too little time. With that being the case as it generally is, why waste time with statistics that don't actually do what you need it to: provide an indication of value and production of your players and/or team? I don't think you should have to. I also don't think you have to look far to find what fat you need to trim, and what direction you need to look to find potential solutions to your problem.

Chapter 13
In With the "New"

Before I say anything else, let me say one thing: When I say "new," that isn't some sort of concession to the fact that new is better, or that sabermetrics are suddenly better and should be ushered in to replace the old way of thinking, despite the whole book prior to this chapter being about us finding a middle ground. What I mean is simply that we should welcome in a new, balanced way of looking at things, utilizing useful aspects of both ways of approaching the game in an effort to see the game more clearly and analyze the game with more precision than was possible while we were in the midst of the figurative Civil War I alluded to earlier.

When I'm going over statistics and attempting to glean some sort of value from all of them, I, admittedly, use a decent amount of the new metrics in addition to plenty of traditional-type statistics. I've found that a lot of times they tell a similar story and, when combined, tell a deeper story than could be told by either by itself. I'm sure no one ever intended for it to be this way, as most people who subscribe to wOBA fantasize of spitting on the shoes of all those grotesque Batting Average fanatics out there, but it's true. Despite the immense and inevitable disagreements that exist amongst baseball people, at the heart of them, all statistics are just trying to figure out who is good and who is bad, and tell that story in a coherent manner.

In my coaching career, and with my apparent title as, "stat guy," which, for what it's worth, I still dispute, I've found a few instances where combining an old statistic with new metrics offer an interestingly unique look at the performance which they're both attempting to quantify. This is not the case with all of them, however, but I have found a good set of metrics that lend themselves to accurately portraying what I value in my players and my team.

If you were looking for solutions to the problems I outlined in the last chapter, look no further! Let's take a look at some of the ways to find balance amidst the madness that is the great statistical war in baseball.

The first adjustment I made to my statistical profile when analyzing my team's performance is that I've begun including wOBA as one of the categories when tracking offensive production. It sits right after AVG, OBP and SLG when I print it out as a full offense chart, so it gives me a nice slash line followed by the stat that, to me, most resembles a slash line in one metric. What I've found is that including wOBA in my evaluations and reports prevents me from being blinded by any one of the statistics included in the slash line. I've had my player with the top Batting Average on the team be number five on the team in wOBA, and I've had a guy with a high SLG have a low wOBA because he doesn't consistently get enough hits to keep his number all that high. wOBA basically condenses all aspects of a player's slash line into one easy-to-read number that also helps with the totally natural inclination to simply put your highest OBP first, highest SLG in the cleanup spot, or plug away based on whatever your personal lineup template looks like. The benefits to keeping both slash line and wOBA don't end there, though.

I've also found that keeping the two stats together also are beneficial in the opposite way. When two players have a similar wOBA, also having their slash line readily available allows me to see *why* the wOBA totals are the same, which gives me a more accurate indication of the type of offensive game they're playing, which allows for more in-depth lineup construction.

For example, a player with the highest Batting Average, but who lacks elite level pop at the plate, may still rank high on the team in SLG simply due to the fact that he gets a lot of hits, and, because he is a good hitter, will run into his fair share of extra-base knocks. At the same time, a player who gets less hits overall (lower AVG), but packs a punch when he does get a hit (higher SLG) may rival him in wOBA rankings when it's all said and done. It helps me in determining where I need to hit each player in the lineup on any given day. A player who is more hit-or-miss, but who is capable of running into a HR or a three-XBH game at any time will likely be more toward the bottom of the "middle" of the order, like five or six, whereas the high volume hitter who has relatively less pop-per-hit but is still extremely productive will probably end up in the two or three-hole, due to the higher likelihood of getting on base. The more consistency also allows me to feel comfortable putting that player in a position in the lineup where he'll likely see a lot of high-leverage AB.

So, as I said, slash line alone may cause me, or another coach/manager to see stars when one of the numbers is extremely high, and miss the overall production value, which is counterbalanced by wOBA. By the same token, slash line allows players similar in wOBA, but different in offensive style to be differentiated between, allowing for a lineup and roster more accurate and conducive to the success of each player because their individual skills set is being put in the best situation to be played up. Obviously, penciling in a player with a high Batting Average in the seven hole will likely require a potentially uncomfortable conversation, but outlining the emphasis on working to that player's skills so that the team is in the best situation to win is imperative to making that conversation productive, and creating the player buy-in to make all that work is a far deeper issue. Maybe in the next book.

The next combination of new and old that I've found creates a unique perspective is another one combining two directly related (and therefore, opposing, go figure) metrics: ERA and FIP.

Now, I know what you're thinking, that I'm out of my mind, and I spent a whole section saying why FIP was *better* than ERA, so how does tracking both of them allow you to see anything? I'd respond by saying that's a fair point. However, I've found the combination allows me slightly deeper inside why the numbers shake out the way that they do.

Let's recap. ERA is "Earned Run Average," or Earned Runs per nine inning pitched, and FIP is "Fielding Independent Pitching," and is basically what a pitcher's ERA would be if they experienced exactly average defense behind them and average luck in terms of borderline balls falling in for hits and hits being strung together against them.

Now, I'm not a big fan of "luck," as it relates to base hits falling in. In my coach brain, I feel that almost everything that isn't a HR can be caught, and if it isn't, our scouting and positioning wasn't good enough. Maybe my coach brain isn't completely logical. Competitive, definitely. Crazy? Well, probably crazy as well. But, for the sake of the argument here, let's go with it and say my coach brain is correct in this instance.

If non-line drive hits falling in are not a result of "luck," and are in fact caused by less than excellent defensive play, then the difference between ERA and FIP creates a unique opportunity to travel through the collective mind of the team while each pitcher is on the mound. Much of the disparity between the various ERAs and FIPs I've seen in my teams have been directly related to the type of pitcher that has been on the mound.

Granted, there have been exceptions. However, generally speaking and almost without fail, the difference between ERA and FIP have been able to be traced back to the pitcher's style and skill. If a pitcher that got a lot of strikeouts was on the mound, more often than not their FIP was even with or better than their ERA. On the other side of the coin, when there is a contact pitcher, or maybe a young pitcher or someone making a spot start on the mound, or perhaps even a guy who generally gets mop-up innings, FIP will usually end up higher than that of their ERA. While this may not surprise you, it has led me to certain ends that have allowed me to shore up my teams defensively regardless of who is on the mound. Let me tell you what I've gathered after many conversations with coaches on my staff, other coaches, doctors, pastors, even a few therapists, anyone who will listen, really.

It appears as though the defense's readiness is affected by the perceived ability of the pitcher to take care of outs on their own. If a pitcher gets a lot of strikeouts and is generally pretty dominant, it seems to almost catch the defense off-guard when the ball is put in play. This creates less than optimal reactions, and borderline balls end up going as hits, either sneaking through the hole or falling a step in front of an outfielder. Over the course of the season, this will generally allow a few more earned runs to score, skewing his ERA to be higher than his FIP.

On the other side of that, if a pitcher has a lot of balls put in play, they rely more heavily on the defense supporting them in order to get their outs over the course of the game. This reliance on the defense keeps strikeout numbers low and in turn will raise that pitcher's FIP. However, the good news is when a pitcher surrenders a lot of balls in play, it generally keeps the defense on their toes and ready to make a play. This is why many pitching coaches want their pitchers to "work fast," or not take a lot of time between pitches. This readiness in the defense could potentially keep an extra ground ball per game in the infield and an extra pop up out of the hit column per game as well. This will *prevent* some earned runs from scoring over the course of the year, keeping ERA down while FIP is skewed slightly higher due to that pitcher's inability to "do things on their own."

Now, keep in mind, ERA is how many runs actually come around to score and FIP is what a pitcher's ERA would be assuming they get exactly average luck and timing. So:

Strikeout Pitcher: Surprised defense = more weak hits/earned runs
More earned runs = **higher ERA**
High K rate = **lower FIP**

Contact Pitcher: Ready defense = less weak hits/earned runs
Less earned runs = **lower ERA**
Low K rate = **higher FIP**

Strikeout pitchers generally receive *less* than average defense because of their ability to handle things on their own most of the time, so their ERA (actual runs) ends up being a little higher than their FIP ("if everything was average" runs). The opposite goes for contact pitchers. The defense is ready to play, so they end up being spared a few earned runs over the course of a season, so their ERA (actual runs) is a touch lower than their FIP ("if everything was average" runs), because they had the benefit of a ready defense to make plays behind them.

What this has led me to understand about these gaps is that when they present themselves, it allows me a quick look into the minds of my defensive players when a certain pitcher is on the mound. It may not necessitate a big, long conversation pre-game, or a 15-minute speech about, "locking it in," during practice (although those inevitably happen), but simply quick cues before or during a game that our guys need to stay locked in on defense. I feel as though I know which pitchers are bailed out by the defense, and which pitchers have to succeed in spite of a sub-par defensive performance. This allows me to both keep an eye on the defense, but also stay in the pitchers' ear about needing to just make pitches if the defense is playing poorly, or that the defense is working behind them so they don't necessarily need to nibble at the corners and risk walking guys.

Now, keep in mind that I understand this gap will generally be larger at the lower levels, and in amateur baseball in general compared to professional baseball. However, as I'll touch on later in the book, the human involvement in baseball is undeniable. The propensity of humans to mentally, "take a play off," even if it's no more than a momentary lapse in focus, exists and will likely rear its head more often when the opportunity to do so exists. In this case, the opportunity exists more when a pitcher is mowing hitters down on their own and the participation of defensive player is therefore lessened, even in the Major Leagues.

If we can go back to the Chris Sale vs. Clayton Kershaw example, we will notice that Chris Sale had a much higher K/9 rate (12.9) than Kershaw (10.4). We can also observe that the higher strikeout pitcher (Sale), had a *higher* ERA than FIP, (2.90 ERA/2.45 FIP) and the pitcher who relied less on strikeouts (Kerhsaw) had a *lower* ERA than FIP (2.31 ERA/3.07 FIP), which would be consistent with our example, while keeping in mind that both pitchers' teams were either first or second in team defensive metrics. Of course, a 10.4 K/9 rate is still very good, but it is objectively not as good as 12.9, so the argument is at least viable based on that example.

So, if you had to choose one way to measure your pitchers' performance, choose FIP. However, that doesn't mean ERA is useless, and that doesn't mean there aren't ways to get an even better look at the inner-workings of your team and pitching than FIP. I've found that keeping both ERA and FIP allow a good look at a pitcher's ability to both handle adversity and pitch to their defense. It also allows me to know which pitchers need a more focused defense behind them, so I don't unknowingly run a team out there that isn't the most prepared it can be for a game. At the end of the day, that is my responsibility. The players play, I need to do what I can to make sure they're prepared to handle whatever will come their way over the course of a full baseball game and season.

The third and final combination of new and old that I've found is one that pertains to defense. As I said, defense is becoming somewhat of a lost art in the modern game, with mammoth home runs and 100mph fastballs captivating the audience more than a backhand in the hole ever could. As a result, young players have devoted less and less time to the development of their defensive game. The amount of high school DHs I see these days is alarming. These are kids that are clearly athletic and coordinated enough to be very good hitters, however, if they don't have a bat in their hand when you throw a baseball their way, it's a wonder some of them can even tie their cleats before digging into the batter's box. I understand that teams will ultimately pay for offense, but those same teams also generally don't draft DHs, so you need to at least be able to play a position to, in my opinion, get on the field consistently. Obviously, I'm in the minority on this issue, but it's how I feel. No teams that ever win at the highest levels are poor defensively. Average maybe, if they hit enough, but you can't give away that many runs on defense and expect to win. But back to my original point, ways to measure said defense.

The reason I said all that was to say this: defense is still difficult to measure. As I mentioned in the DRS section of the book, "range," as it relates to defense, is highly subjective and mostly imaginary, but it's what plays a huge role in measuring defense in today's game. Especially in amateur baseball, the capability to collect range data and turn it into usable information is beyond most programs, and even if it weren't, I'd still have to drag and edge the field before I even worry about setting up a range data collection system. So, allow me to suggest a somewhat simpler means of measuring defense.

I mentioned it in passing during the DRS section, but I've found that, in a pinch, using both Fielding Percentage and Range Factor (per game or per nine innings, I use per seven innings because high school games are seven innings) provides a good look at the ability and production of a defender. Again, Fielding Percentage is simply the amount of plays made (Putouts + Assists) divided by total chances (Putouts + Assists + Errors). Range Factor is just the average number of Putouts and Assists a player will have over the course of a game. Range Factor can be calculated per nine innings or per total game, and both are easy to calculate. I choose per seven innings rather than nine because I think it just keeps things uniform with a lot of other statistics that I keep and it scales them down to a more accurate look as to how they compete in the high school game.

Now, Range Factor is not exactly cut from the same new-fangled and algorithm-based cloth as the likes of WAR, DRS or wRC+, so that may make it a little easier to digest for those who may fear weighted metrics like they're the boogieman here to haunt their baseball dreams. It has emerged as a more popular metric as of late though, while Fielding Percentage is a dinosaur as far as statistics go. So, there is a sense of old vs. new in this combination, and I think it's the most bang for your buck in terms of getting a good look at a player's defensive contributions.

The reason for my thought process behind using both Fielding Percentage and Range Factor to look at defenders is that it basically tells you everything you need to know without the hassle of finding a way to combine a bunch of different metrics into one, as would be the case with DRS. It takes how many plays you make per game, an indication of range (Range Factor), and how consistently you're able to convert the balls in play you get to into outs (Fielding Percentage). This allows me to see how many plays a player can be counted on to make during the course of a game, but in addition I also see how consistently their chances to make plays are converted into outs. So, if a player is making a lot of plays, which leads to a high Range Factor but are also making a lot of errors, it stands to reason that their errors are likely due to expanded range and them having a play on balls other players at their position don't get to. That, I can live with and will just work on either being smarter with throws or actively work on ranging them out during practice. On the other hand, if a player has a very good Fielding Percentage but has a low Range Factor, it can be determined that they are not making a lot of plays relative to other players at their position, so we need to work on reads or jumps. Now, of course there is value to making all the plays within a small range, but obviously the more range the better if all else is equal.

I've been working on finding a way to combine these two to quantify both aspects of measuring defense into one number, but haven't found a way that I like yet. I've tried simply multiplying Range Factor by Fielding Percentage, essentially breaking down Range Factor by the percentage of chances they convert into outs. So if a player has a Range Factor of 4.00 and a Fielding Percentage of .975, I'd simply go with 4.00 x .975 = 3.9 as a final adjusted Range Factor. I'm not sold on it, simply because most Fielding Percentages are between .950 and 1.000, so the degree to which the Range Factor is affected wouldn't create any kind of significant separation. I've also toyed with the idea of simply subtracting their adjusted Range Factor as found above from their original Range Factor and multiplying by 100 present it more neatly. So, using the example above:

$$\begin{array}{r} \text{Original RF} = 4.00 \\ \underline{- \text{ Adjusted RF} = 3.90} \\ \mathbf{.10} \\ \underline{\text{x} \quad 100} \\ \textcircled{\mathbf{10.0}} \end{array}$$

Or:

$$\begin{array}{r} \text{Original RF} = 4.26 \\ \underline{- \text{ Adjusted RF} = 4.19} \\ .07 \\ \underline{\text{x} \quad 100} \\ \textcircled{7.0} \end{array}$$

The thought process behind that is to essentially outline who has the smallest disparity between their original Range Factor and their adjusted Range Factor, but that way doesn't account for the original value of the Range Factor itself, which obviously matters because the amount of plays you can make per game matters in terms of your defensive value. Back to the drawing board I go!

To sum all this up, Range Factor by itself is a good measure of range, but doesn't lend itself much to consistency, while Fielding Percentage is a good indication of consistency, without much mention of range. Combining the two allows you to see both the amount of balls a defender gets to during the course of a game, and also the frequency with which that same player is able to convert chances into outs. If you recall during the DRS section, I also outlined taking note of the rates with which certain teams induce ground balls or fly balls may also play into measuring a defender's contribution. This accounts for potential outliers which generally come by way of unusually high ground ball or fly ball rates and can skew a player's Range Factor. This is also an easy fix.

I simply mark down all batted ball types on the scorecard I keep during games. "G" for ground ball, "L" for line drive and "F" for fly ball. Here is an example of what my card would look like (Again not asserting that you should do it this way, but just to give you an example):

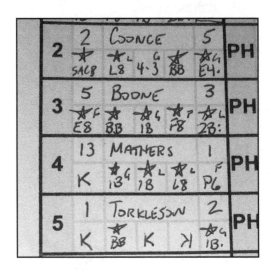

So, as you can see, in the top right corner are all types of batted balls in play (bunts excluded). Again, I mark either a "G" for ground ball, an "L" for line drive, or an "F" for fly ball. The rest of the markings I make are to keep track of other things during the plate appearance. Overall, keeping track of batted ball types aren't that difficult if you're already keeping a book during games. This allows me to see our rates and compare our rates to other teams, as I keep the same card for our opponents.

These types of measurements allow me to, as I said, know how many various types of batted balls we hit during a game, and how many of the same types of batted balls our opposition hits. This gives me a general feel for the "average" ground ball, line drive and fly ball rates for our pitchers, and in turn allows us to compare against other teams and aids us in seeing how well our defenders are making plays based on how many opportunities they get. This isn't a perfect substitute for the league average statistics that are kept for Major League games, but their means of data collection and mine don't even exist on the same plane of reality.

I can't send scouts to every game in the state of Oklahoma and see what the ground ball rates are, however, I can see if our pitchers are getting more ground balls than the pitchers we face. That allows me to at least see how our rates stack up against the teams we play, which is honestly all I'm concerned about anyway. I'm not worried about how we compare to the teams we don't play, so if league average in my case literally means "opposition average," then that's more than okay with me.

The only issue here is that this doesn't exactly work for catchers, as they have many more factors to be graded on, but the amount of runners they throw out attempting to steal in tandem with their passed balls and wild pitches will give you a good idea of how they perform. I'm working on some metrics for catchers too, so don't touch that dial!

So, again, combining Range Factor and Fielding Percentage, two defensive statistics that fight for mainstream baseball statistical supremacy, can actually work together to create a much more in-depth look at any player's contributions with the glove.

I know it seems counter-intuitive to take two stats about which people constantly debate as to the truly superior option and use them both in tandem, but I've found that a lot of times it really helps to broaden the view of the measurements in question. Statistic and metrics, traditional and sabermetrics, they're all just trying to do the same thing, so taking the good from both to cover the flaws of both generally clean things up in a hurry and offer some unique insight as to the details that are right under your nose as it relates to the game playing out right before your eyes.

Consider Chapter 13 to be my final effort to bring the people together. I want so badly for all the constant in-fighting to end because I feel as though it is impeding progress. All told, all the theories, statistics, algorithms and everything else are all trying to do the same thing, so why are we trying so hard to prevent each other from doing that? If anything, this section is living proof that old statistics and new-age metrics can co-exist. Not only that, they can be combined and, in many instances, actually *improve* the overall clarity with which we see performance. Who woulda thunk?

Well, I mean… I would have. Hence the book.

Regardless, it's still a thought that I'm certain hasn't occurred to many people, which is the main reason I felt compelled to write this in the first place. I've offered all the information and perspective I can, so at the risk of forcing you to read more of my droning on, I'd just like to take this opportunity to throw away the research, stop crunching numbers and simply talk about some of the things that I see in the game today and offer my two cents on them.

PART 6

Some Things To Get Off My Chest

In this section, I'm going to take the opportunity to address some things that I feel need to be said in regard to the direction in which the game has been moving in recent years. They are not necessarily statistics or metrics, more just concepts or theories that I think need to be laid out in a coherent manner. And no, four guys in suits at a desk arguing about them is not a coherent manner. Not that they're wrong, but the issue with debate is when it comes to certain subjects (in today's baseball, it seems like they're all sore subjects), the conversation only causes people to be more deeply engrained in their side of the argument, more defiantly sticking to their guns in the face of scrutiny of their position. This is not conducive to collaborative thought.

I feel as though it's important to take a good look at all the ideas being tossed around in today's game. From pitch clocks to computerized umpires, launch angle to "swing down," and everything in between. A lot of what has been offered up spells the end of mainstays and institutions in the game of baseball. I just feel as though changes of that magnitude need to be closely examined from all angles, not just from the angle that an umpire missed a call in a big spot, so now everyone's pissed and wants to bring on the robot umps every time it happens.

Again, not to say the new suggestions are wrong, but baseball has been subject to significant mass-outrage over a variety of topics over the last few years, so I would be remiss not to point out that as violently as public opinion can be swayed in this age of social media and the immediate dissemination of information, we need to be sure that we're absolutely positive that we want what we're crying out for, especially given the degree to which some of them may alter the game as we know it.

So, if I may, I'd like to offer my thoughts on a lot of the hot-button issues in the game of baseball today.

Chapter 14
"I'm a person, too!" The Human Element in Baseball

Obviously, baseball is a human game. Created by humans, played by humans and officiated by humans. So why then, are we as a community gradually (and ever-more rapidly) moving toward edging the human influence out of the game? I'm all in favor of continually tightening up the accuracy and flow of the game, however, I feel as though every time a human element is removed, the game loses a bit of its luster. Whether it's umpires, replays, pitch clocks or anything else, it's a slippery slope to eliminate human influence, because so much of the game is reliant on it.

The argument that we need robot umpires has been circulating in many baseball circles, and I could not be less in agreement. Human umpires have been a part of the game since its inception, and they have become as instrumental in the marketing of the game as most players. The issues that would arise from having sensors in place of a man behind the plate would be enormous, as would the effect on the marketability of the game.

We've all seen it thousands of times: An umpire calls a strike on a pitch that the batter thinks is a ball, and they begin to chirp. The umpire ends up ringing up the batter on a similarly close pitch and the batter loses it. The two men get nose to nose and are yelling at each other and then...

It happens.

He makes the motion so oft-replicated by die-hard and casual fans alike. The sweeping arm motion, as if to literally throw the batter out, into the parking lot on the other side of the wall separating the third deck from the outside world.

"You're gone!"

"You're outta here!"

"That's it, get out," or any other phrase umpires like to use. The umpire ejects the batter. After that, the manager comes charging out from the dugout and tosses the player aside, because now he wants a piece. His face, red with anger, jaw clenched, vein protruding from his forehead and all, he begins to mirror the actions of the player, screaming in the umpire's face until, he too, is ejected. The stadium crowd erupts. Fans, throats coated in Bud Light, are screaming from the crowd,

"Throw him out!"

"Toss him!"

"See ya, Skip!"

It's a spectacle combining equal parts passion, competitiveness and immaturity, and it's a type of dust-up that doesn't exist anywhere outside of baseball (and maybe WWE). Do we really want to lose that because sometimes we get mad that Joe West calls a strike on a pitch that's a baseball-width off the outside corner? I don't.

How many times have there been extremely boring, uneventful Major League Baseball games? For the record, I don't find baseball games of any kind boring, but sometimes they are uneventful. Either way, you know the kind, the final score is 1-0, there were four combined hits between the two teams and every last one of the 27 outs recorded by each team came of the routine variety. Those highlights never make it on the 11 p.m. broadcast.

Unless.

Unless someone got mouthy with an umpire over something seemingly insignificant. The game that may otherwise be completely devoid of any entertainment value to the casual fan is instantly ratcheted up to primetime-level entertainment. If you think that doesn't go a long way in marketing the game, you're crazy. For example, I know tons of people who watch hockey only to watch guys punch each other in the face. Is it overly-primal and confusing to me? For sure. But, to each his own, and some people will watch baseball just on the off chance he gets to watch a 50-something-year old former player blast spittle all over the face of a 60-something-year old umpire from point-blank range. Not to mention, you can't convince me that the confrontation and disagreements will cease if robot umpires are introduced.

Regardless of whether there's a human being back there or not, if a pitch is called a strike that a player doesn't think is a strike, there will be pushback from the player. It's inevitable. So, instead of a player blowing off steam at the umpire behind the plate, what will the player have to do? Refuse to leave the batter's box to go sit in the dugout? Will it come to the point where the player channels that inner-child that exists in all ballplayers, as we mentioned before? Will he throw the kind of tantrum that would motivate even the crankiest toddler, and proceed to sit crisscross apple sauce on top of home plate until the MLB recalibrates its obviously defunct machine? Who knows?

You may be scoffing, but I've seen enough baseball – and baseball players – to know that almost nothing is below them when it comes to expressing displeasure with the way the game is being called. During the 2018 season, I watched a 67-year old Butch Hobson (former Major League player and former manager of the Boston Red Sox) remove the third base bag and give it to a young fan in the stands and, later in the same month, take a dry swing and proceed to trot *all the way* around the bases in protest of calls made by umpires as the manager of the Chicago Dogs of the independent American Association.

Now, I played for Hobson in 2016, so I loved every second of his tirades, and personally bore witness to a handful of incidents in which his emotional cup had runneth over, but the fact remains: objection and demonstration of said objection have become almost a performance art as it exists in baseball. If you think umpires without a pulse will put a stop to that, I think you may be in for a rude, and potentially expensive, awakening, depending on the location in which they plan to place this robotic umpire. As we've seen over the years, players are not always shy about taking their bats to objects other than baseballs when they feel so inclined.

Of course, that's not to say that umpires are without faults of their own. As a former player and current coach, I've had my run-ins with plenty of umpires that have no business being on a baseball field. I've experienced guys who clearly, and I mean *clearly*, have some self-esteem issues or other things that need to be ironed out and who weren't afraid to impose those issues on anyone and everyone in attendance of the game they were calling. That isn't different in Major League Baseball, and probably even worse so, with players constantly calling out umpires for "making the game about them." I don't necessarily even have a problem with those assertions, because I've seen it first-hand. However, the umpires' presence is as much a part of the game as the players, and I'm sure some umpires would rather not have to deal with certain players either, especially the ones who spend most of the AB criticizing their calls.

Obviously, the umpires concern is a somewhat small blip on the radar when it comes to prevalent issues within the baseball community. There are other more pressing issues at the forefront of the minds of Major League Baseball's powers that be. However, the human element remains in the crosshairs, as many of the front offices in the league have turned to analytics-exclusive approaches which have condensed a player – a human being with complex physical, emotional and environmental profiles – to mere data. While I do understand some of the benefits to the analytics sector's influence, I think in this case, it's missing the mark completely.

When ignoring the fact that your players are actual people, you lose sight of some of the intangible aspects to their game or presence that can positively benefit a team. When it comes to evaluating players, ignoring their humanity and treating them as entries in a spreadsheet would seem to indicate that the more sophisticated method of evaluation is the one that is less thorough. There are so many things that go on in a player's life over the course of a season or career that don't show up in the box score, but still have an enormous effect on performance.

For example, the analytics movement prides itself on being able to accurately project performance. So, would the José Bautista, Josh Donaldsons and Justin Turners of the world have had a career post-age 29 had the machines taken over just a few years earlier? In an age when uber-prospects are getting younger and younger and front offices are valuing young talent of whom the team has control for many years before arbitration/free agency as much as ever before, it's possible that all three of these players in their *very* late-20s, with several years of service time and without producing to the point of making themselves stand out, may have been overlooked in favor of these younger players. If you look at the pre and post-age-29 splits, all three of these players were pedestrian to, perhaps, on the upper end of average at best in the seasons leading up to their age-29 season. However, since then, all three have taken off and have had stints during which time they have been among the best in the business.

For insight:

Pre-Age-29 Season[19]							
Player	*G*	*AVG*	*OBP*	*SLG*	*wOBA*	*HR*	*RBI*
José Bautista	575	.238	.329	.400	.321	59	211
Josh Donaldson	405	.268	.347	.458	.353	63	228
Justin Turner	318	.260	.323	.361	.305	8	89

Post-Age-29 Season							
Player	*G*	*AVG*	*OBP*	*SLG*	*wOBA*	*HR*	*RBI*
José Bautista	1,214	.251	.373	.505	.383	284	762
Josh Donaldson	469	.280	.382	.546	.399	117	317
Justin Turner	609	.306	.385	.506	.388	84	311

As you can see, all three players saw a significant uptick in production after their 29th birthday which, by today's standards, just as a golfer walking onto the tenth tee box, places them definitively on the back nine of their careers. In other words, they are in the latter half of their playing days in Major League Baseball. Justin Turner played the fewest games before turning 29, with his total of 318 being just under two full seasons' worth of games. However, his age-29 season was in 2014, and he had seen time in the Major Leagues in every season since 2009, so he had already been around the league for quite some time.

---

[19] Via Baseball Reference

My point of showing you these numbers is that, more than ever, Major League Baseball's front offices and the way they evaluate players is a strictly, "What you have done for me lately," type of business, and perhaps even more so, "What can you do better than someone else in your pay-grade for the next two or three seasons?" When players are being called up and having an impact in their very early 20s, even sometimes as teenagers, the value on club control and roster manipulation by executives is as important as ever, which makes the market for 28-year olds with three or four years of service time who are still trying to find their swing increasingly miniscule. Teams have strayed from the seven or eight year (or more) contracts because, as many of us could have predicted, they end up being worth it for the first three or four, and then players get older, the team gets worse because all the payroll is locked up on one guy into next decade or the player simply has more money than he knows what to do with and loses a little edge, and production begins to dip. Sometimes, the player struggles and never receives that contract in the first place.

The most recent age-29 season of our three examples was that of Josh Donaldson, whose age-29 season was in 2015. However, I think we can all agree that the game has changed significantly since then. Many of the metrics, theories and buzzwords that are commonplace today either hadn't been concocted yet or were still in beta phase around the league. Donaldson was also probably the most successful prior to his 29th birthday, but his production post-turning 29 so far exceeds his totals before that they don't even appear to be from the same player. Generally by 29, a player has his style and approach down and you can get a good feel for the kind of production to expect from him. With less value being placed on the "eye-test" in recent years, a 30-year scout saying, "That Donaldson kid is one adjustment away from being special, his makeup and work ethic graded high when we signed him, so let's see how he plays out," might not be accepted with the same weight as one of the Player Development Department's 26-year old human calculators saying, "Based on his past and current production, his age and our projections, and [insert laundry list of contributing factors], I feel as though he has reached his peak production and is not worth extending,

I recommend trading for prospects or designating him." Or something along those lines, I've never sat in on one of those conversations, so an accurate representation of the verbiage generally used eludes me.

Either way, as a result of that, a team may have moved on from Donaldson in favor of a younger, more athletic and more malleable-to-the-team-approach prospect, and missed out on a now-MVP player and one of the most feared hitters of the last three or four seasons. Same goes for Bautista and Turner. Guys who today would be cast aside for their low-wOBAs or less than desirable WAR totals would be selling insurance today instead of either being one of the most well-rounded hitters on one of the most prolific offensive teams in the National League (Turner), or being an American League HR champion and author of arguably the most memorable bat-flip in this game's history (Bautista).

What I'm trying to say in regard to these three players is simply that players are not raw data that you can plug into a formula and simply calculate their value. There are external and internal factors that are inherently human and cannot be quantified. I'm not saying that using these metrics and algorithm-based measures as *one* part of player development and evaluation is bad, because as I've stated throughout this book, I believe using these numbers and advanced analytics has benefits that don't exist in using other methods. With that being said, I'm also saying regarding analytics and these progressive measures as the *only* part of the evaluation process is short-sighted and misses an entire, large faction of what makes up a player.

There are a million reasons a player's production may slip in a given year. They could have had a baby at the end of March and are sleeping terribly, or maybe they have a nagging injury, but don't want to disclose it in order to stay off the Disabled List, or to create the stigma that they are "injury-prone" with looming free agency. Maybe they were traded and had to move to the other side of the country, leaving their families behind. Maybe there is some sort of family tragedy, anxiety or some other type of situation that is on their mind that people don't see. None of it will be met with mercy when it comes time to re-negotiate contracts, and it shouldn't be. However, a player may be placed pre-maturely on the downward slope of their career arc if they have a misstep at 28 years old, as could have been the case with Bautista, Donaldson and Turner. And as we know, losing them at 28 meant not having them at 29 through the present, when their contributions have become significant.

The human element is ever-present in our game and its value is the same reason I feel that WAR can't accurately depict a team's propensity to win. The "whole is greater than the sum of its parts" factor comes into play, especially in regard to a team. There's chemistry that comes into play, relationships, communication and a myriad of other factors that all cannot be, and are not, quantified. It's also why certain players remain on big league rosters long after they are productive every-day, or even utility, players. Their ability to influence the other human beings in a clubhouse to improve that chemistry, communication and overall team morale by simply being there, going about their business like a true professional is invaluable and has earned many players an additional few million dollars in the last few seasons of their career. It's called veteran presence, and it's one of the largest examples of the importance of honoring the human element in our human game.

One benefit that can be brought about by a player other than their contribution on the field is that which they bring by being a contributing member to the team chemistry. This is a particularly impactful contribution, and more marked in regard to the disparity between human effect and analytical value, when the player begins to lose some of their physical ability, usually due to injuries, old age or a combination of one causing the other. There are many instances, now and in history, of an older player not exactly moving mountains on the field, but can act as a mentor or beacon of professionalism to the younger, more talented prospect-types in the clubhouse, creating a positive work environment more conducive to their and, in turn, the team's success. Veteran presence is a real thing, and many guys have had jobs for years beyond their peak productivity because of it.

For a prime example of the benefits veteran leadership provides, look no further than everyone's favorite "Grandpa": 2016 Chicago Cubs' catcher David Ross. The nickname, "Grandpa" is obviously in reference to Ross' age in relation to the most notable players on the team. He was given the nickname by two of the faces of the franchise at the time, Anthony Rizzo (then-26 years old) and Kris Bryant (then-24). Despite being used mostly as Jon Lester's personal catcher, and otherwise spelling then-rookie Willson Contreras, Ross' impact on the Cubs' clubhouse went far beyond giving young players a breather.

Ross is a zero-time all-star, a zero-time Silver Slugger, zero-time Gold Glover, zero-time Hank Aaron Award winner, zero-time MVP, and two-time World Series Champion. Oddly enough, the managers of the World Series teams he played on cited him as one of the primary contributors to the team's success. Now, I understand the role of field manager is being slowly edged out of the game, with pitching match-ups and strategic moves essentially being spelled out by the analytics department, which allows teams to hire managers who have, in some cases, never coached anything... ever... to run their ball club so they can pay them nothing, saving salary for a high-performing analytics department (more on that in a minute), but there's no way both of his managers, John Farrell (BOS '13) and Joe Maddon (CHC '16) are dummies.

In 2013, David Ross played in 36 games as, "...more than a backup, but not a starter," as Red Sox then-manager John Farrell stated, serving generally in a role as second fiddle to every-day catcher Jarrod Saltalamacchia. In those 36 games, he slashed .216/.298/.382, with four HR, 10 RBI and 11 BB to go with 42 K, posting a WAR of 0.8, less than one win above average and making about four times the league's minimum salary. Less than spectacular, no? However, Ross' impact laid primarily in what he did behind the scenes.

He and pitcher Jon Lester developed a strong bond to the point that he eventually became Lester's personal catcher during their World Series run in 2013, meaning that every time Lester pitched, Ross was behind the plate calling the game. As we know, Lester has become one of the best big-game pitchers in baseball, and has three World Series rings of his own (2007 & 2013 with Boston and 2016 with Chicago). So, Ross had a calming influence on one of the team's top pitchers to the extent that he didn't want to throw to anyone else. In addition, Ross had an influence on two Red Sox rookies, just a couple pups in their early-20s by the name of Xander Bogaerts and Jackie Bradley, Jr., now-mainstays in the current Red Sox lineup. Ross also brought that influence with him to Chicago when he joined the Cubs, starting in 2015.

Despite hitting a big HR in Game Seven of the 2016 World Series, his on-field contributions, while legitimate, pale in comparison to the intangible value he brought by simply being there. His presence spurred on the younger Cubs players and showed them what it means to be a true professional. He influenced young players such as Kris Bryant, Anthony Rizzo and Jason Heyward, so much so that after the Cubs pulled out the win in Game Seven of the 2016 World Series, the latter two carried Ross off the field in true hero's fashion. All that for a "backup" catcher, but why? Look at his WAR! Look at his OPS+! Look at his Batting Average!

Look no further than the way he's spoken about by the people around him.

Cubs' manager and zen-master Joe Maddon referred to Ross as the "heartbeat" of the 2016 team that broke the franchise's 108-year World Series drought. A player that had only been on the roster for two years, and had played sparingly during that time. The fact that he was regarded as highly as he was and was thought to contribute *so* much, despite, on paper, not really contributing a ton shows the value of leadership and intangible benefit of the way human beings can affect one another. That's because what happens on the field is only a small portion of what happens over the course of a Major Leaguer – or any baseball player's – day. Mentoring young players, acting as an extension of the coaching staff or simply just conducting business as usual and imprinting on young players unknowingly are all things that are the responsibility of older players, and are factors that will never show up in the box score and will never be available on the back of someone's baseball card. And it doesn't end at David Ross.

Juan Uribe was signed by the Cleveland Indians and took it upon himself to mentor the young players, especially young Latin players, ones who may not have spoken much English, who were attempting to acclimate themselves to Cleveland, Ohio. Despite hitting only .206 in 73 games in 2016, his presence shone through two young players who became every-day Major Leaguers for the first time that season, and, by this time, chances are that you've heard of them. Their names are Francisco Lindor and José Ramírez. Uribe's influence was such that people began joking that he and Ramírez were father and son.

Yet another example of this would be that of Chase Utley in Los Angeles, for the Dodgers. A former all-star and MVP candidate with the Philadelphia Phillies, and a player who certainly could never be cited for lacking hustle, Utley, 39, continues to cast a shadow in Los Angeles that extends to their minor league affiliates in Oklahoma (Double-A, Tulsa and Triple-A, Oklahoma City). There are stories of minor league coaches telling their players to keep their noses clean and handle their business because, "Utley is watching." His intense, looming presence can be felt throughout the organization and has impacted minor leaguers and young Major Leaguers alike. "Super-utility" player for the Dodgers, Kiké Hernández, has consistently joked about being Utley's son throughout the 2018 season, even at one point posing for pre-game pictures with Utley and his actual sons as one big, happy, Utley family. Again, Utley is 39, despite what his silver hair says, and Uribe was 37 in 2016 when he drew his "dad" jokes, so obviously the father reference is a loose one, but their influence is felt to be nearly as strong as that of an actual father by those experiencing it. Being new to anything is a struggle, but when you hear horror stories of rookies' experiences when they are first called up the Major League club, you can imagine the sense of security that a veteran taking you under their wing would provide and the benefit that could have on a young, budding player. Don't get me wrong, the dad jokes are definitely funny, but the meaning and influence that exists for those jokes to even be made is something that needs to be taken into account when determining a player's true value.

Whether it's "Grandpa Rossy," the uber-intense Chase Utley, or anyone in between, the presence that can be felt by a player who isn't contributing at an elite level on the field is undeniable. That impact is one that cannot be overstated, and seemingly every winning team has a veteran player that provides this type of leadership (Justin Verlander for the 2017 World Series Champion Houston Astros, for example). Verlander may actually be a bad example because he happens to still be filthy, even at 35 years old, but veteran leadership is veteran leadership, my point is statistical production is different than intangible leadership, and they're both equally important and impactful, despite what a computer may say. It would appear that leadership of that type may be on its way out, with teams insisting on keeping their roster air-tight, and with no glaring production gaps. I'm not convinced of the fact that this would be a positive for the game of baseball. With that in mind, the same argument could be made with the recent influx of rookie managers being given the reigns of a Major League team in recent years. Are established veteran managers becoming obsolete as well?

Recently, a lot of young, inexperienced coaches have been given managerial jobs for Major League franchises. Before 2018 alone, five managers have been hired who have never managed in the Major Leagues before. The Philadelphia Phillies hired Gabe Kapler, the New York Mets hired Mickey Callaway, the Washington Nationals hired Davey Martinez, while the New York Yankees brought Aaron Boone on board and Boston Red Sox filled their vacancy with Alex Cora. Now, not to say any of these men are unfit or that I don't think they'll do a good job, because that's not the case. All I'm saying is an unprecedented number of Major League teams are entrusting their rosters to men who have never fulfilled the duties of the position they've just been entrusted to carry out. Aaron Boone was hired out of the broadcast booth, with no coaching experience and Kapler has never coached in the Major Leagues (he managed a Class-A affiliate in 2007 and served as a Director of Player Development for the Dodgers for the three seasons prior to his being hired as manager).

Although I'm not sure if it's ever been said out loud, it appears to me that this isn't merely happenstance and that it didn't just so happen that of the six new managers hired for the 2018 season, five of them had never managed before, and beyond that, they all were hired to manage teams that were either coming off a postseason appearance in 2017 (WAS, NYY & BOS), or were expecting to emerge from the depths of a rebuild soon (NYM & PHI). I believe that front offices are believing that a manager doesn't necessarily need to be a lifer like a Bobby Cox or Tony La Russa to be able to manage (I don't believe that either, as all lifers were rookies at one point, just maybe not all at once), but that they simply need to be able to read numbers handed down from analytics and be able to apply them in a game situation. Whether or not this is the case, individually or universally, it appears that things are at least headed in that direction, and I believe that is a mistake for the same reason releasing David Ross before 2016 would have been a mistake.

If you have a great sense of what players are a good matchup against a certain pitcher, that's awesome. How do you get them to show up and grind out a 10-pitch at-bat and give everything they have in game 160? There's no formula for that, you need a manager that players want to show up and play hard for. You need a manager that knows when to poke the bear and when to back off and let a player work through their struggles. A manager needs to be able to motivate and regulate tempers, egos and personalities while consistently having a feel for the ever-changing pulse of the clubhouse, in addition to their duties of writing an effective lineup and making the right moves in-game. You can't just drop Johnny Somebody in the manager's office, hand him the numbers and expect him to be effective, no matter how fluent he is in the language of analytics. Even if a lot of your job happens on a baseball field, when you're in charge of a room full of dozens of human beings, the work goes far beyond plugging and chugging based on what the numbers say. Maybe a guy is banged up that day. Maybe a guy has pitched two days in a row so, even though the matchup works in his favor, his compromised stuff may lead to a less-than-favorable outcome. These are all things that have to be taken into account and I'm not completely convinced they always are.

Managing a big league team is the ultimate dance, dealing with multi-millionaires who expect certain things, keeping them happy, keeping them in a rhythm on the field, while attempting to get role players in the game and seeing what young guys are made of when thrown in the fire. Guys will be removed from the starting lineup, guys will be optioned to the minor leagues and guys will be traded, and it takes someone with elite people skills to navigate these sometimes murky waters. If front offices plan on simply installing a figurehead who can read numbers and will pledge allegiance to those numbers as it relates to their in-game moves, they will run the risk of hiring someone who could potentially be unable to fulfill half or more of their job description. Again, not to say any of the new hires are unable to do anything required of them, I'm simply making the point that one-sixth of all Major League teams just hired someone who has never done that job before, so I feel as though my speculation is at least justified based on the sheer quantity of new hires.

When the dust has settled on this revolution, whether you want to oust human umpires, or don't care if a guy is a good leader if his numbers are low or that a manager is merely a figurehead, I think you are missing out on an enormous part of what makes the game of baseball so great. The human element is something that may not be tangible or visible to the eye, it may not show up in the post-game box score and it may not even be something that we can nail down and fully understand, but to assume that because of that it's simply not there and *must be eliminated* is off the mark, in my opinion. After lots of thinking about this, I've found that the human element and leadership, as it exists in baseball, is basically the traditional view's version of WAR. We're not really sure *what* it is, tough to figure out exactly *how* it works or *why* it works, but it does! It makes sense and players, managers and GMs swear by it in their process of filling out rosters. As it pertains to umpiring, I just firmly believe that we will miss their presence and the spectacle that occasionally accompanies their presence. Not to mention, kids coming up in the game will still be dealing with human umps and then will be dropped off in Double-A with KIT from Night Rider's cousin calling balls and strikes and not know which way is up anymore. But that's beside the point. Humans play the game and I think the influence that has on the sport needs to be honored and appreciated more than it is. Plus, if managers and coaches are on the way out, I'm out of a job!

Chapter 15
The Ghost of Statistics Past: Views from the Island of Misfit Metrics

S tatistics have been a part of baseball culture since the game's inception in the late 1800s. Since then, many statistics have been created and have inevitably, albeit nobly, died on their shield attempting to assign value to things that baseball fans and statisticians alike simply did not want to, or feel the need to, know about. I feel that this fact could be taken into account a lot more today, given the current climate of the game. People are in a panic that these new metrics will be around forever or that the traditional statistics will soon be lost to history. Rest assured, folks, that many statistics have tried to gain entry to the elite club of mainstream Major League Baseball statistics, and many have been denied. Not every metric or statistic that has been created and introduced has stuck. As with anything, failure is a part of baseball, developing statistics is no exception. I've even tried to toy around with creating statistics or metrics of my own (although I think the main culprit of their failures is that I'm probably just not good enough at math), but that's not the point!

The point is that statistics come and go just like players do in this game, so there's no need to fear. Let's talk about just a few of the statistics that were briefly accepted in baseball but have since failed the test of time, vanishing away somewhere into the archives of baseball to collect dust for eternity. I'd like to start with the Hold.

The Hold is essentially the Save for set-up men. It's a way to quantify contributions made by relief pitchers who are not the closer. Now, before I even start, this statistic would die tomorrow if it didn't a while back with the way teams currently deploy their bullpens. Many teams use the "all hands on deck" model where all pitchers are fair game all the time, regardless of situation. Assumed "closers" are no more, with a team's best one-inning reliever sometimes being used in the sixth inning, with someone else nailing down the ninth, depending on when the highest-leverage situation occurs during a game. But back to Holds. Holds are essentially measured the same way as a Save, except that a pitcher can amass one in any inning that is not the last of the game.

A Hold is given to a pitcher if that pitcher:

1. *Enters the game in a save situation; that is, when all of the following three conditions apply:*
   (a) *He appears in relief (i.e., is not the starting pitcher) when his team is leading; and*
   (b) *He is not the winning pitcher; and*
   (c) *He qualifies under one of the following conditions:*
      (i) *He enters the game with a lead of no more than three runs and maintains that lead for at least one inning*
      (ii) *He enters the game, regardless of the count, with the potential tying run either on base, or at bat, or on deck*
      (iii) *He pitches for at least three effective innings.*
2. *Records at least one out;*
3. *Leaves the game before it has ended without his team having relinquished the lead at any point and does not record a save.*[20]

So, essentially, if a pitcher comes into the game with, at most, a three-run lead, records at least an out and doesn't relinquish the lead, he is credited with a Hold. Multiple pitchers can get a Hold in a game, but one pitcher cannot receive multiple Holds. Again, this is a way to attempt to quantify the contributions of the frequently un-thanked middle relief pitcher. This was especially useful a few years ago, when every team's bullpen was hyper-organized, much *un*like today's game.

---

[20] MLB Official Info

Every team seemingly had their starter go seven innings, then throw their eighth inning guy (set-up man) and then their closer for the ninth and *whaddaya know?* The game is over. The starter gets a W, the eighth inning pitcher gets a Hold, the closer gets a Save and all is right with the baseball world.

However, the Hold never really caught on, as it isn't regarded as an official Major League Statistic, despite it showing up on TV broadcasts not too long ago. I remember specific instances when now-Dodgers pitcher Ryan Madson was the setup man for closer Brad Lidge in the back-end of the Philadelphia Phillies' bullpen during their winning years of the late '00s and early '10s. He would enter the game and the graphic under his name would display his Holds. While I liked and still like Ryan Madson, I could never really get into Holds, and apparently I wasn't alone.

The Hold was invented in 1986 and simply never took strong hold as an accepted statistic. It still exists occasionally and shows its face on some websites' leaderboards and maybe in fantasy baseball, however it simply was unable to take hold and captivate the world as the new statistic on the block. The reasons why are beyond my understanding, but a guy can wonder…

Perhaps Holds too closely mimicked the Save, and ended up just telling fans when a pitcher was able to "save" the seventh inning. I can understand the lack of drama of being able to "save" the game when it's 4-1 in the sixth, as opposed to finishing off the ninth inning to secure the win. Ultimately, Holds required the same things as a Save, but simply lacked the necessary magic surrounding the accomplishing of the necessary tasks. I would definitely understand if that were the underlying reason that Holds didn't hang around.

Maybe the Hold just seemed like a last-ditch effort to bring a little glory to the middle relievers. Middle relief pitchers are generally what offensive lineman are to football: undeniably important, but also incredibly un-sexy. There are no high-stakes, bases loaded, two outs, with the other team's best hitter at the plate with the game on the line-type moments when you only pitch to left-handed hitters in the sixth or seventh inning. While no one can deny that having effective middle or even late-relievers is vital to a team's success, they simply are not starters and they simply are not closers. Casual fans want starters to strike out 10 hitters over eight innings and then for the closer to come in and pump 100mph heaters so we can get to the fireworks show after the game. And in a world when the game caters to the casual fan (looking at you, pitch clocks), starters and closers remain the rock stars of the staff, so they get the recognizable statistics next to their name. It's marketing. Is it fair? Probably not, but it is marketing.

To be fair, I too would much rather watch all-time Saves leader Mariano Rivera unleash 94mph turbo-cutters and shatter three different guys' bats like plywood in a karate tournament than see Arthur Rhodes pitch a spotless seventh inning. I don't need a stat to tell me that Rhodes did his job, because he came in with the team winning, and he left with the lead intact, and that's good enough for me, and I assume that was good enough for the rest of the fans out there, inevitably leading to the demise of the Hold forever.

For reference, Arthur Rhodes is the all-time leader in Holds (since Holds started being officially kept), with 231. Not to belittle his accomplishments, because he pitched over 20 seasons in the big leagues and even being a warm body on a big league roster for that long is extremely impressive, and just a warm body he was not. Not that he cares what I have to say about his outings or anything anyway, but, just in case anyone thinks I have anything against Arthur Rhodes, 13-year old me greatly appreciated his contributions to my Phillies in 2006.

Anyway, the other resident of the Island of Misfit Metrics is the ever-important Game-Winning RBI.

What's Game-Winning RBI?

Glad you asked.

Game-Winning RBI, which will henceforth be referred to as "GWRBI," was a statistic that was officially-kept by Major League Baseball from 1980 to 1988. It measured exactly what the title indicates: the amount of RBI a player collected that drove in the game-winning run, regardless of inning. A player could get a GWRBI in the first inning just as easily as he could by walking a game off in the ninth. So, to give a hypothetical for demonstration:

If a game is tied at 3-3, and a player gets an RBI in the fifth inning that pushes the score to 4-3 in favor of his team, and the team goes on to win without ever again relinquishing the lead, that player would be credited with a GWRBI.

That sounds great!

It gets better.

To alter our original hypothetical: Imagine the player puts his team ahead 4-3. His team then extends their lead to 8-3, and eventually goes on to win the game 8-7. The player that drove in that fourth run *still* gets credit for the GWRBI, despite his RBI not actually being the one that ended up being the difference in the game. However, his RBI did put the team ahead and the team didn't ever give the lead back up, so, GWRBI for Billy Sevenhole. And so began the issues with GWRBI.

Why would the player who drove in the fourth run get the GWRBI, when the player who drove in the eighth run is the one who drove in the run that *actually* represented the difference in the game? It doesn't really make sense. It only makes sense in the sense that I understand what they were going for when introducing this statistic in the first place. The execution is simply not practical.

GWRBI was a statistic introduced to me by my dad many years back, and even when I was 10 years old, I remember thinking, "What in the world were they thinking?" The simple fix would have been to amend the measurement of the GWRBI by saying:

"The player who drives in the run that puts the winning team's final run total above that of the losing team shall be awarded a Game-Winning RBI," or something along those lines.

In other words, if we look back at our original example, had Billy Sevenhole (goes without saying, but, he doesn't exist) driven in the fourth run to make it 4-3, and then his team added insurance runs to make it 8-3, gave up a four spot in the ninth but still hung on to win 8-7, Billy wouldn't get the GWRBI because his fourth run wasn't the one that separated his team from the opposing team. It was an important run, as is the case with any run in the event of a one-run game, but it wasn't the game-winner. The GWRBI would go to the player who drove in run number eight: Jimmy Twospot. For those of you asking, no, Jimmy Twospot did not appear in the movie *A Bronx Tale*.

However, had Billy Sevenhole driven in the fourth run, making the score 4-3, and his team simply added insurance and won by a score of 8-3, Billy *would* have received credit for the GWRBI, because his RBI accounted for the run that put his team above the opposing team, while Jimmy Twospot had to live with a measly regular insurance RBI.

Yeah, that would have been better. But that's not how it was.

Instead, Billy Sevenhole gets all the glory no matter how much heavy lifting Jimmy Twospot, Cleanup Carl or Stevie Late-inning-defensive-replacement do to actually put the team on top, and because of that, GWRBI was not effective at portraying that which it set out to portray and was rightfully vanquished from the Kingdom of the Almighty League of Statistics with Staying Power.

Game-Winning RBI encountered and suffered the same fate as the Hold, not because it was a stat that nobody really cared to know, but because the way it was measured was astronomically and unfathomably impractical. I think I speak for the significant majority when I say that I believe we all would like to know how frequently a player drives in the run that puts his team up for good. I think it would've been a good first step in attempting to quantify what I believe to be the un-quantifiable: the clutch factor of a player. Beyond that, though, it simply would be a good, quality statistic that I believe would have had legs as a way to measure which players are able to come through in tight situations, or who simply have a knack for putting the nail in the coffin when their team has a lead, both enormously important aspects of being a good player and characteristics all good teams have. Timely hitting and putting teams away late in games matter, period. GWRBI should matter, but it doesn't because it was built on a rocky foundation and that's okay, I guess. Former Mets 1B and, and one of the faces of the "Borderline Hall of Famers Club," Keith Hernandez is probably bummed because from 1980-1988, he has the most GWRBI ever with 129. He'll have to settle for his 1B-record 11 Gold Gloves.

The purpose of discussing the untimely demise of Holds and Game-Winning RBI is not to mock "dumb" statistics that people don't care about, that's not what I'm out to do. It was simply a means of illustrating the point I've really been trying to make all along, which is that statistics come and go, some are great and some are bad and they're all up for interpretation and they all have or had some sort of perceived value, at least at some point or another. The fact that some of these numbers were considered to be valuable at one point clearly doesn't mean they remained that way, and same goes for the statistics that are sweeping the nation now, or the older ones that have been around for a long time.

The fact that new ways of viewing player production have been introduced is not something to be scared of, especially not to the point of debate. No one is trying to destroy the game. If GWRBI and Holds teach us anything, it's that the lens through which we view baseball is ever-changing and will likely never stop changing until the final out is recorded for the final time. The developers of WAR are attempting to help the game just like people who swear by Batting Average, and whatever ends up working the best will stick. Everyone thought that Game-Winning RBI was going to be the new cool stat on the block that would be used for decades and centuries to come, but when I introduced it, I could literally hear people saying, "What is a Game-Winning RBI?" through the pages of this book. C'est la vie. Like sands through the hourglass, so are the statistics of our game (changing the words, not the vibe).

Maybe one day, people will stop using Defensive Runs Saved, or maybe one day people will come to agree that a pitcher's W/L record is merely a place holder on the back of their baseball card, and shouldn't carry much weight in terms of analyzing performance. Either way, people have been trying to quantify the smallest aspects of baseball since long before Bill James ever picked up a pencil. The fact that these modern developments in player performance measurements have built up a head of steam may mean they're doing more good than harm, although understandably some of its main proponents are insufferable in terms of smugness; I will give you that. However, the same could be said for some of the former players who stand on the opposite end of the spectrum, unable to be budged from the mindset of the era in which they played. It's all a balancing act, and we as a community have been doing the dance for over 100 years, so this new wave of change is only different in that there are perhaps more x-values to be solved for this time around.

Conclusion

I decided to write this book when I heard highly respected baseball people, on a television network that will not be named, arguing on baseball topics. I know what you're thinking and, trust me, I understand that that's the format of 99% of television programming anyway. However, it wasn't the argument so much as what they were arguing about that truly bothered me.

I watched men in suits, with their extensive baseball resumes listed on the screen under their face, enlarged to fit my TV screen (although it could be argued the figurative head sizes may have actually been scaled down, based on the way they were talking), argue about statistics. Statistics.

"We're talkin' 'bout statistics, man!"

In the middle of a Major League Baseball season, which never fails to provide interesting story lines, grown men who are trusted to provide meaningful baseball insight for a successful television network are sitting on my screen talking about whether x is better than y, and why *aaaanyone* who thinks such-and-such statistic is relevant must be a fossil themselves, etc. Meanwhile, somebody was probably in the middle of a 10-K, complete game shutout or hitting for the cycle. It's a complete waste of time.

Dean, your whole book is basically that conversation.

Sure, to a certain extent. The difference being I feel as though I've offered an unbiased look at both sides of everything I've brought forth in this book, whether I liked it or not. The other difference is that I don't kick down your door and sit in your living room talking to you about it during primetime viewing hours. I wrote a book because that way people who *want* to know will be able to receive this information at their own will, pace and timing.

As I said, I don't write this book expecting it to propel me into baseball-intellectual status, or to support any professional endeavors of mine in any way. I simply saw a hole in the game, and felt like I had something to offer in service of fixing it. That's it. I believe we spend far too much time debating on who's right and who's wrong and not nearly enough time discussing how we can use certain metrics and statistics together and how much better we could make the game if we simply tried to make the game better rather than make ourselves right.

Hasn't the NBA taught us anything? Kevin Durant to the Warriors? LeBron joining Wade and Bosh in Miami? It's easier to work together than butt heads for years and years (too soon again?). Don't get me wrong, I love competition. However, what is the sense in competing if there is no contest? From where I stand, it just seems silly and that's exactly what all these Hall of Fame players, former GMs, Directors of something-or-other and professional journalists are doing on a nightly basis.

If we as a community put forth half the effort in attempting to better our game as whole as we did on proving the bad guys on the other side of the wall wrong, well, I'd have nothing to write about and this book would have never existed. But that's okay. That's why I'm writing the book. I love baseball and I want to see it flourish. There is already a marketing problem in the game as it is, and we're not helping our case by spending our time, efforts and resources to show why wOBA is better than Batting Average or why wRC+ needs to chill with all the uppercase, lowercase and special characters going on in that name. It's pointless, and we have much more pressing issues at hand, if you ask me.

Mike Trout could walk into a room and most people, and more than likely almost all non-baseball fans would think, "That guy looks strong, he should play sports!" Meanwhile, LeBron James is one of the most recognizable faces in the world. It can't just be because of LeBron's greatness (though he is great), because Mike Trout's performance relative to his peers is comparable. It's because Ernie Johnson and Shaquille O'Neal don't spend halftime shows talking about why FG% is dumb and we should focus more on Plus-Minus or start using acronyms to analyze player's on-court performance. They don't do that because it doesn't do any good. They brand their talent as a means of branding the game, and they don't waste time fighting with each other about menial things like statistics.

When it's all said and done, people are going to use what statistics they view as useful anyway. There is no sense in trying to convince me that a certain statistic I like to use is dumb, because, firstly, I didn't ask you. Secondly, I think it's valuable, so your thoughts on it don't really influence the fact that, based on the way I view the game, I think a certain statistic is important to take note of. Besides simply being arrogant, it's a waste to try to convince someone of your side, because opinions are opinions, and time will tell anyway, so everyone would do better to contain the smoke pouring from their ears.

Baseball is truly a beautiful game. As I've said before, I think it offers an incredibly unique set of life lessons and creates a very self-aware person. Baseball people, more than "people" of any other sport, tend to view life in a far more big picture way, and tend to not take themselves so seriously, most likely because their whole lives have been rooted in failure. Self-deprecating senses of humor aside, I find it so weird that baseball people are fighting tooth and nail for their preferred side of the argument because I've never known baseball people to sweat the small things to such an extent.

"Oh, you don't like what I think about that? Sounds good, I'm just trying not to go 0-4 tonight."

There are hundreds, if not thousands of different statistics, metrics and measurements present to quantify baseball performance. And guess what? They're all okay, I promise! None of them bite, and none of them are inherently bad or are set out to paint the game in a negative light. And as I've shown, a lot of them actually agree when not looked at through the scope of a rifle. So, everyone hold your fire. Drop your weapons. Cease and desist. Take a step back for just a second take a look at the battlefield around you. It's your brothers and sisters. We all want the same thing, so stop trying to tear one another's heads off before we render ourselves incapable of solving the problems we've created or we render our game a sideshow debate with broadcasts of baseball games airing in between. I want what you want, unless you want an argument. I speak in allegiance to the game of baseball, and nothing else, and I encourage you all to do the same. Our game deserves everyone working as hard as they can to find the best way to see it and present it to the world, not the best version of *your* way to see it, so you can post on Instagram or get some face time and talk about how much better you are. It's not about you. It's not about me. All I'm asking is for everyone to take a look at how silly we appear arguing so rabidly, and over what? Statistics that measure a game that requires hitting balls with sticks.

I've given you all I can give you. Both sides of stats I like, metrics I don't, vice versa and everything in between. If one person reads this and finds it useful and beneficial, great! If not, it still felt good to say all of this. It is my sincere hope that we come to appreciate everything that this game has to offer, even if we disagree with it. It's all useful if you know what to look for, so maybe we should fight for that.

In parting, I would like to sincerely thank you all for hearing me out over the course of however long it took you to get to this point. I find all aspects of the game of baseball to be captivating and amazing in its own right, and I hate to see sensible people lose their minds arguing over things that are as arbitrary in the grand scheme of things as statistics. They're numbers, the game happens on the field anyway, let's try to enjoy that.

So, I've asked it once, and after presenting every bit of information I could, as unbiasedly as I could, I ask of you, my faithful baseball friends, once again:

Can't we all just get along?

Appendix

In many of the chapters of this book, I referenced players, teams and particular instances that were taking place during the 2018 Major League Baseball season. At the time I concluded writing the book, the 2018 season was still in progress, so many of the statistical examples that I used had yet to be finalized by the completion of a full season. However, the season ended in the time between the conclusion of my writing and its release to the public, so I wanted to give a look at how our 2018 examples ended up faring on a full-season scale and see if they would still be viable examples in the sections which they were used.

I wanted to see if over the last couple months of the season, the statistics regressed or the severity lessened, or the disparity in the examples grew. The 2018 season was one that was very polarizing in terms of how the game was managed and played, and the divide was ultimately what spurred me to write this book. We saw players hit under .200 and continue to be every-day players, we saw strikeout - as well as home run - numbers that were historically high, and we saw possibly the highest number of infield shifts the world has ever known. Regardless of your personal stance on any of these things, they need to be closely examined and I think the best way to do that is not rely on numbers pulled from a season that had yet to be finished. Generally speaking, a full 162-game season tends to iron out any potential outliers, so I tend to trust what even one full season says in terms of statistical production and reliability of the statistics in question. Obviously, our 2018 examples were incomplete, and thus more prone to outliers as of the original writing of the book, but they are completed now.

So, again, let's take a look at the 2018 MLB season and see how our examples look now that they are etched in stone.

Chapter 4: Pitcher Wins Take the "L" (Jacob deGrom)

Jacob deGrom of the New York Mets was a perfect example of the shortcomings of looking at a pitcher's wins and losses to determine their production value. At the time of the original writing, deGrom was 8-8 in 26 starts despite sporting a 1.71 ERA. His domination did not falter in his remaining six starts of the 2018 season. He finished with a 1.70 ERA, with 152 H, 46 BB and 269 K in 217 IP. His per nine IP rates were 6.3 H/9, 1.9 BB/9 and 11.2 K/9.

His final record was 10-9.

If you recall, the other example used in tandem with deGrom was Luis Severino of the Yankees. Let's compare their final statistics for 2018:

Pitcher	ERA	FIP	IP	H	BB	K	H/9	BB/9	K/9	*HR/9*
deGrom	1.70*	1.99*	217.0	152	46	269	6.3	1.9	11.2	1.2
Severino	3.39	2.95	191.1	173	46	220	8.1	2.2	10.3	1.0

*league leader

Severino went 19-8.

Again, Severino had a very good year, and this isn't to take anything away from him, it's just to put in writing that pitching wins aren't indicative of how well a pitcher is performing. deGrom was better in basically every single category, yet had nine less wins and nine more losses, which had the potential to harm his Cy Young case.

Fortunately, deGrom enjoyed the same success as Felix Hernandez in the postseason awards voting, winning the National League Cy Young Award, sporting the lowest wins total for a Cy Young Award winner ever, with 10 victories on the season, despite his otherwise utterly dominant 2018 campaign.

Despite his dominance, there was one voter – one – who didn't give deGrom a first-place vote.

The voting finished as follows:

Pitcher	First Place Votes	Vote Points
Jacob deGrom	29	207.0
Max Scherzer	1	123.0
Aaron Nola	0	86.0

So close to a unanimous Cy Young nod, yet so far away. Realistically, Max Scherzer had a tremendous year as well, despite a shaky final few starts raising his ERA, but he still led the league in IP and K. I honestly thought the voting would be much closer, with deGrom ultimately still winning in the end. So you can make your own judgment, the final statistical breakdown for the three Cy Young finalists looked like this:

Pitcher	W-L	ERA	FIP	IP	K	BB	ERA+	BB/9	K/9	*HR/9*
deGrom	10-9	1.70*	1.98*	217.0	269	46	216*	1.9	11.2	1.2
Scherzer	18-7	2.53	2.65	220.2*	300*	51	168	2.2	10.3	1.0
Nola	17-6	2.37	3.01	212.1	224	58	175	2.5	9.5	0.7

*league leader (among starting pitchers)

Considering deGrom led the league in ERA, FIP and ERA+, while Scherzer led the league in K and had a higher IP total by 3.2 over de-Grom despite a difference of only one K/9 (12.2 for Scherzer to 11.2 for deGrom), I would have to believe that his 10-9 record was the only thing that prevented him from receiving the Cy Young unanimously.

In addition to that, if we return to the deGrom/Severino comparison and take the run support Severino received and gave it to deGrom, there is a legitimate chance deGrom could have gone undefeated. The Yankees average 5.25 runs per game in 2018, so in theory, five runs surrendered had a chance to win every game. Luckily for deGrom, he never even gave up more than four. In every single start he made in 2018, he held the opposing team to four runs or less, which would put him in a position to secure the win, assuming he had that 5.25 runs of support. 32-0 sounds outrageous, like you're playing a video game, but based on deGrom's dominance, he had as good of a chance as anyone in history to pull it off if he had a team capable of scoring more runs.

I doubt he would have actually gone 32-0, or that a pitcher will ever go undefeated. Not the least of the reasons for that being that the trend appears to be that starters will not be going the necessary five innings to secure a win as much as in the past. But generally, things happen, teams score runs late, have an outlier-type game and get shut out, etc., so losses are going to happen, which is yet another reason that they are unreliable, but that's beside the point. A pitcher may never go undefeated through a full season in which they make over 30 starts, but Jacob deGrom pitched about as well as a guy can, and still didn't have the wins to show for it. That is mostly because wins don't show much in the way of pitcher performance.

While it is exciting and refreshing that deGrom received such over-whelming voter support in the Cy Young voting, there is still at least one holdout out of the 30 eligible voters, which means there are still many holdouts across the baseball world. We are coming closer to rec-ognizing the flaws in pitcher wins and losses, which is a good start. At the very least, we have to recognize the flaws, even though the voter recognition has trended significantly in the right direction.

Chapter 9: Make ~~love~~ wins, not WAR (Washington Nationals)

The 2018 Washington Nationals were a team that, on paper, looked like a favorite to compete for a National League Championship. Great hitters like Bryce Harper, Daniel Murphy, along with teenage-sensation Juan Soto proving to be a pleasant surprise, posting a slash line of .292/.406/.517 with 22 HR and 70 RBI as a 19-year old. Pair that with a pitching staff including perennial Cy Young candidate Max Scherzer in addition to maybe the scariest number two starter in the league in Stephen Strasburg, the Nationals seemed to be sitting pretty before the start of the 2018 season.

However, as I said before, the game isn't played on paper. It's played on dirt.

The Nationals underachieved, going 82-80 in a season that many picked them to represent the National League in the World Series.

Despite that outcome still likely being lower than their desired win total, adding their players' total WAR had them going 87-75, which is five whole wins greater than their actual record for the season. Keep in mind how large a gap five wins is in terms of value throughout a roster. Some notable five-WAR players in 2018 were:

Five-WAR players	
Nolan Arenado (COL)	38 HR, 110 RBI, 4th in UZR, 3rd in Def. RAA
Javy Báez (CHC)	.290/.326/.554, 34 HR, 111 RBI,
J.D. Martinez (BOS)	.330/.402/.629, 43 HR, 130 RBI
Aaron Nola (PHI)	2.37 ERA, 3.01 FIP, 212.1 IP, 224 K

WAR essentially credited them with the value of any one of these players on top of the team they already had. Again, it's basically stacking an MVP or Cy Young candidate on top of your roster and having a man up on the opposition all season long. However, they were not that good. WAR didn't account for whatever it was, be it leadership, culture, or just sheer bad luck that led to the Nationals ultimately barely scraping by to exceed a .500 win-loss record for the year.

As we stated, WAR does a good job, but it can sometimes overlook the inherent human elements or intangible qualities about the game that can be large factors in a team's success. Baseball teams and their seasons are not able to be simply plugged into a formula and crunched, spitting out their value, etched in stone based on the expectations of a reading. It's far more complex than that, even more complex than the many already-complex-enough algorithms and formulas that go into WAR, which go over my head as it is.

Chapter 10: "Save" me the trouble: What exactly is DRS? (Freddy Galvis)

San Diego Padres' SS Freddy Galvis has been victimized by DRS in the past, with the metric far undervaluing his defensive contributions since years before he arrived in San Diego. He is consistently a top-five or ten finisher in just about every defensive category on a yearly basis and has found himself in the cellar of DRS leaderboards on multiple occasions. While 2018 saw a slightly more accurate representation of Galvis' defensive production, I still don't see how his DRS total is ranked worse among league leaders than any of his other statistics:

Freddy Galvis 2018						
G at SS	*A*	*PO*	*Field%*	*RF/9*	*Team GB%*	*DRS*
160 (1)	399 (6)	222 (2)	.986 (2)	3.99 (7)	44.4% (9)	7 (8)

Total (MLB Rank)

Despite finishing no worse than seventh in Major League Baseball in any defensive statistical category, he still finished eighth in DRS. He actually led the league in games played at SS and was second in baseball in PO and Fielding Percentage, and despite his team inducing ground balls at the ninth-highest rate in the game, he still had the seventh-highest Range Factor/9 total.

His average finish among the five statistical categories is somewhere between third and fourth. Yet, somehow his DRS ranking is eighth. I'm not entirely sure what it is that is having such a negative impact on his DRS totals, maybe it's Arm Runs Saved or "Picking on You Just Because" Runs Allowed that is acting as the primary detriment. Either way, despite Galvis finishing more in line with his actual production this year, it would still appear that he is undervalued by DRS.

Chapter 11: Not All Parks are the Same, so Why Level the Playing Field? (Arenado/Hosmer)

In Chapter 11, I detailed how players who play at Coors Field in Denver, Colorado, namely 3B Nolan Arenado, have their production unfairly diminished because of the high altitude of their home ballpark. In making my point, I discussed how many players in Major League Baseball perform better at home than on the road, even those who play in traditionally pitcher-friendly ballparks. My example was new San Diego Padre as of the 2018 season, 1B Eric Hosmer. When Hosmer's production was illustrated in the chapter, his season had not yet been completed, so let's see if a full season evened out what appeared to be a discrepancy in park effects' argument that players in hitter-friendly cities have an unfair advantage.

As a reminder, Hosmer's disparity between his home and away splits were greater than that of Nolan Arenado in all categories listed other than SLG as of the original writing:

Nolan Arenado	G	AVG	OBP	SLG	H	2B	HR
Home	438	.320	.374	.609	536	124	108
Away	438	.263	.318	.469	439	98	78
% Home Production	*50.0%*	-	-	-	*55.0%*	*55.9%*	*58.1%*
Home + / -	-	*+.057*	*+.056*	*+.140*	-	-	-

Eric Hosmer	G	AVG	OBP	SLG	H	2B	HR
Home	79	.284	.357	.449	86	20	10
Away	78	.223	.287	.348	69	11	8
% Home Production	*50.3%*	-	-	-	*55.5%*	*64.5%*	*55.6%*
Home + / -	-	*+.061*	*+.070*	*+.101*	-	-	-

Granted, Hosmer hasn't played as many games in San Diego as Arenado has in Denver, so it's possible that their production could change and possibly even out as the years go on. However, the charts above clearly display that Hosmer is generally not only better at home than on the road, but his production generally has a larger gap between home and road games than that of Arenado.

"% of Home Production" is simply an indication of how much of a players production takes place at home vs. on the road. As you can see, more of Hosmer's production came at home than Arenado's. With the exception of HR, which Arenado hits 2.5% more HR at home than Hosmer, and SLG, where Arenado's home/away split exceeds that of Hosmer by 39 points, it would seem that playing in a hitter-friendly park hasn't given Arenado much of an edge over a player in a pitcher-friendly park, as Arenado's road splits are somewhat comparable to Hosmer's home splits.

Obviously, one example doesn't make a case to completely over-throw anything, but the fact that some of these metrics and approaches to analytics are sold and presented as air-tight, and that they are able to give a perfectly accurate look is simply untrue in this particular instance.

With the 2018 season being over, we can now objectively see that all of the instances which were used to illustrate the pros and cons of various measurements and approaches held up down the home stretch of the season. In some cases, pairing the 2018 season examples with examples from the past have been able to show that some measure-ments have never really been beneficial. I'm very curious to see how 2019 will pan out. A lot of new approaches and strategies have been placed under the microscope due to their increased usage during 2018; will this increase the amount of infield shifts? Jack up strikeout totals in the ongoing search for HR? Will we see a season with zero sac bunts and zero SB attempts?

Only time will tell.

CPSIA information can be obtained
at www.ICGtesting.com
Printed in the USA
BVHW081239220419
546167BV00025B/1599/P

9 781949 231922